Magical Folkhealing · Libraries

Discover magical wisdom that has been passed down through generations in this guide to using herbs for spiritual, emotional, and mental health and healing. Packed with natural remedies and recipes from D.J. Conway and her grandmother, this book is a magical formulary that anyone can use to make life better.

Magical Folkhealing features a variety of herbs and provides their associated planet, element, deities, and zodiac signs, as well as their basic powers and specific uses. This beginner-friendly handbook also teaches you how to simplify your rituals, use special tools and tables for improved prep work, apply oils and aromatherapy for specific needs, and much more. From herbal teas and tinctures to massage oils and stones, this guide is an indispensable resource for healing.

The Sun rules all operations involving employees, p‐
friendships, healing, divine power, labor, would lea‐
The Moon rules spells dealing with the home, family,
cooking, clairvoyance, medicine, dreams, the sea.
Mars rules all operations of conflict, hunting, surg‐
physical strength, courage, politics, debates, athletics,
competition and rituals involving men.
Mercury rules rites involving studying, learning, tea‐
divination, predictions, self-improvement, communic‐
every kind, the mind, celibacy.
Jupiter rules all rituals of wealth, poverty, monetary
legal matters, honors, luck, materialism, expansion
Venus rules all operations of love, pleasure, art, musi‐
and perfume composition, partnerships, rituals involving
Saturn rules those operations concerning buildings, r‐
funerals, wills, reincarnation, destroying diseases and
eliminations and death.

Raw Materials and Correspondences
Agrimony to Saturn; Bay to the Sun, sometimes Jupiter; B‐
Mars; Eyebright to the Sun, occasionally to Venus or Merc‐
to Mercury, occasionally the Moon; Galangal Root to Jupiter
authorities say Mars; Grains of Paradise to Jupiter; Lavend‐
though sometimes to Mercury; Marjoram to Mercury; Oak t‐
sometimes to the Sun; Orris to the Sun, sometimes Jupiter
to Venus; sometimes to the Moon; Rhus Aromatica mainl‐

---

d apple blossoms to
3 pieces, sub each one sick of
pieces. The decaying apple will ease ‐
not is done with warts. Use apple cider in p‐
one; if they are called for in old magical spells
at apples on Samhain. Apples are sometimes also
‐‐ or the poppet.
‐‐ (Arbutus unedo)
‐‐: Strawberry Tree
Cold
Moon
t: Water
Deities: Dis, Khensu, Neith, Diana, Luna, Morrigan
Used: Berries
c Powers: Divination
‐ific Uses: At one time in Ireland, where the shrub grows
fusely, the berries were eaten or made into a narcotic wine
or visions and prophecy.
Aromatic Bush: See Cal‐
Asterisks: See Mugwo‐
Asafoetida (Ferula ‐‐
Gender: Hot

---

in a definite altered state. Excessive amounts
VERY DANGEROUS.
Maté: steep the leaves in hot water and drink as a ‐
and other pisines. A very good stimulant and ‐
the system as coffee.
Mandrake: brewed as a tea by boiling the crushed root. Said to have a
very strange narcotic and hypnotic effect. Prolonged use not
recommended. VERY DANGEROUS.
Mormon Tea (Ephedra): boiled in water 5-10 minutes, steeped, and then
drunk. Acts as a stimulant, also relieves congestion and asthma.
Morning Glory: LSD-like experience lasting about 6 hours. VERY DANGEROUS.
Indian (Virginia) Snakeroot: lowers blood pressure and tranquilizes
the mind without causing stupor and ataxia. Effects last
for several days.
San Pedro Cactus: similar to peyote but more tranquil. Takes 1 to 1½
hours to come on, lasts about 6 hours. DANGEROUS.
Sassafras: tea in large doses as a stimulant and induces perspira‐
tion. A hallucinogen. Aphrodisiac in large doses, euphoriant
in small doses.
Skullcap: brewed as a tea. Effective as a no‐
quiet and sooth those wi‐
Valerian: ‐‐ tea before ‐‐

---

y usually to the Moon; Rue to Saturn; St. John's Wort (Hypericum)
‐ury; Southernwood to Mercury; Valerian to Saturn, some say
‐; Verbena to Venus, possibly Mercury; Willow, Witch Hazel
‐rmwood, all to the Moon.
Oils and Spices
‐‐d to Venus; Ambergris to the Sun; Aniseed to Mercury; Cassia
Sun, sometimes to Mercury; Civet to Saturn; Ginger to Mars,
‐ly the Sun; Khol, as this is a mineral, possibly to Saturn;
‐‐ and Lime to Mercury; Mace to Mercury; Mandarin to the Sun;
‐ to Saturn; Nutmeg to Venus, possibly to Mercury; Patchouli
‐‐s in his Sign of Scorpio; Saffron to the Sun or Jupiter;
‐dalwood (White) to the Moon, but sometimes to Mercury;
‐dalwood (Red) to Venus in her Sign of Taurus; Ylang Ylang to
Moon or Neptune.
Gums, Resins and Balsams
m Acacia to the Sun; Gum Asafoetida to Saturn; Gum Copal
‐ Jupiter; Gum Dammar to Mercury; Gum Elemi to Venus;
‐libanum to Jupiter; Gum Karaya to the Moon; Olibanum to
Moon, often the Sun; Opopanax to Mars; Scammony Resin,
‐‐‐ Root to Saturn; Storax to Mercury
‐‐‐‐ Tragacanth to

Magical Folkhealing

About the Author

A native of the Pacific Northwest, author D. J. Conway has studied the occult fields for more than thirty-five years. Her quest for knowledge has covered every aspect of Paganism and Wicca to New Age and Eastern philosophies plus history, the magical arts, philosophy, customs, mythologies, and folklore. In 1998 she was voted Best Wiccan and New Age author by *The Silver Chalice*, a Pagan magazine.

Conway is the author of more than twenty nonfiction books, including *Celtic Magic* (Llewellyn), *Dancing with Dragons* (Llewellyn), *Mystical Dragon Magic* (Llewellyn), *The Ancient Art of Faery Magick* (10 Speed Press), and *The Little Book of Candle Magic* (10 Speed Press).

She lives a rather quiet life, with most of her time spent researching and writing.

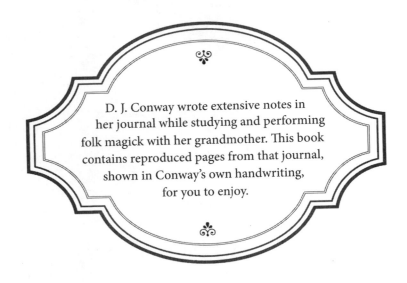

D. J. Conway wrote extensive notes in her journal while studying and performing folk magick with her grandmother. This book contains reproduced pages from that journal, shown in Conway's own handwriting, for you to enjoy.

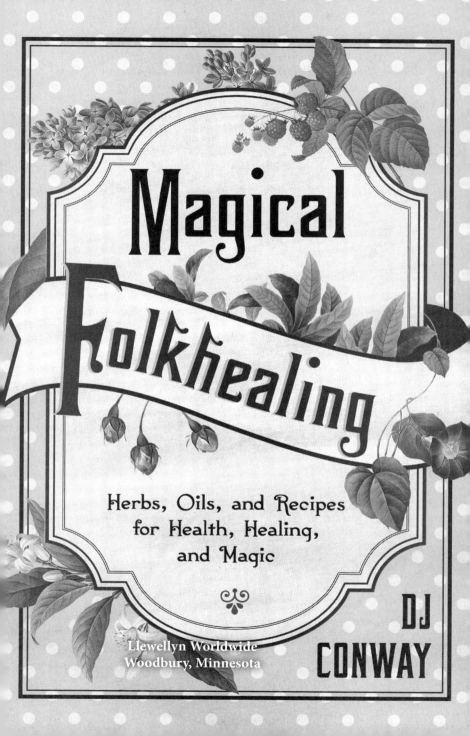

Magical Folkhealing

Herbs, Oils, and Recipes for Health, Healing, and Magic

❧

Llewellyn Worldwide
Woodbury, Minnesota

DJ CONWAY

FIRST EDITION
First Printing, 2019

Book design by Bob Gaul
Cover design by Shira Atakpu
Editing by Laura Kurtz

Llewellyn Publications is a registered trademark of Llewellyn Worldwide Ltd.

Library of Congress Cataloging-in-Publication Data (Pending)
ISBN: 978-0-7387-5754-4

Llewellyn Publications
A Division of Llewellyn Worldwide Ltd.
2143 Wooddale Drive
Woodbury, MN 55125-2989
www.llewellyn.com

Printed in the United States of America

Dedication

This herbal is dedicated in memory of my grandmother Clara Fern Long née Corbin and David Hann Sr. Hopefully, people will find it useful in this fast-running, topsy-turvy, uncertain new century.

..., as the scent of
...ove operations an...
Geranium — Affo...
...se and protect a ...
Is also put on the ...
...'s fear, and promot...
...rary — One of the mo...
...ism. It can be put o...
a house, and is used ...
...racts peace, health, pr...
...ower, and courage. Aids...
...illow induces ...

Specific ... charms, as incense...
for evocation, scrying, dur...
Once burned in all incenses designe...
clairvoyance and divinatory incenses (especially...
with mugwort) as well as in exorcism and protection w...
onto fires on Samhain (Halloween) to gain protection from the spir...
roaming the night. Burn while using a pendulum.

Yarrow (Achillea millefolium)
Folk Names: Seven Year's Love, Sanguinary, Old Man's Mustard, Mili...
Herb, Old Man's Pepper, Soldier's Woundwort, Knight's Milfoil,
Nosebleed, Thousand Seal, Hundred-Leaved Grass, Millefolium, N...
Arrow Root, Eerie, Ladies' Mantle, Knyghten, Wound Wort, Stanch
Field Hops, Tansy, Gearwe, Noble Yarrow, Yarroway, Devil's ...
Devil's Plaything, Achillea, Snake's Grass, Death Flower, Sta...
Gender: Cold
Planet: Venus
Element: Water
Assoc. Deities: Venus, Aphrodite, Hathor, Freya
Parts Used: Flowers
Basic Powers: Love, Clairvoyance, Exorcism
Specific Uses: Used in divination spells and to consult the...
Sleeping with a bag of yarrow under one's pillow gives...
one's future spouse. Was a witches' herb. Used in ma...
and marriage charms, as it has the power to keep a c...
happily for 7 years. Worn as an amulet, it wards of...
Held in the hand it stops all fear. It is sometimes...
exorcism incenses. Considered a sacred plant with spiritu...

Yew (Taxus baccata)
Folk Names: Chinwood, English Yew, European Yew
Gender: Cold
Planet: Saturn
Element: Earth

..._Dill Weed_ — gets its name from the Old Norse word "dilla" (mean...
I suspect peppery scent reputed to be soothing. Pungent sc...
when used with mint, citrus and woodsy ingredients.
Eucalyptus — pungent, with a slight medicinal scent.
Frangipani — warm, rich, exotic oil.
Gardenia — heady, sweet fragrance is a symbol of secret love.
Grapefruit — fresh, citrusy odor.
Heliotrope Implode — blend well with citrus and vanilla-like sce...
Hyacinth — fresh, tangy floral scent. A symbol of corrupt love...
Jasmine — symbol of sensuality, from Persian word "Yasmyn". Th...
seductive scent; heavy and sweet. Blends well with rose, other...
and Oriental perfumes.
Labdanum — heavy, sweet scent very popular in Victorian times. Co...
from the resin of a small wild shrub of the mountainous coasts
of the Mediterranean. Fragrance is rich, herbaceous and balsa...
Blends well with the earthy and animal-like scents such as patchouli
and musk. Also used as a fixative in many verbena and violet-type
perfumes.
Lemon Grass — fresh, lemony and aromatic.
Lilac, Blue — symbol of first love; scent of summer rain.
Lilac, White — symbol of innocence; strong, full-bodied aroma.
Lily of the Valley — sweet, penetrating bouquet. Blends well with roses, violets and
orange blossoms.
Magnolia — delicate fragrance.
Mimosa — richly-textured oil with honeyed undertones.
Muguet (French Lily of the Valley) — delicate and lovely.
Musk A — a strong, basic aroma.
Musk X — exotic natural smell.
Myrtle — symbol of love and immortality; sweet, herbaceous oil.
Blends well with bergamot, clary sage, lavender, rosemary, bay.
Narcissus — comes from the Greek "narkaō" (to be stupified). Sweet,
earthy fragrance. Symbol of egoism.
Nutmeg — spicy aroma.
Orange, Bitter — comes from the peel of the almost ripe fruit. Spicy,

...st incense...
...mote the Sight.
...ne — Gives hope to one wh...
...enard — Wear during situ...
..., also to anoint sacred o...
...anctis — A good oil for th...
...tes determination. Also...

WICCAN NAME	COMMON NAME
Dove's Foot	Cranesbill
Dragon's Claw	Crowley Root
Dragon's Eye	Nephalium Loganam
...gonword	Bistort
...'s Foot	American Mandrake
Smoke	Deadly Nightshade
...'s Plant	Fumitory
Star	Elecampane
...ng Fingers/Cloves	Vervain
Five Finger Grass	Nosebleed
Flesh and Blood	Foxglove
Fox Tail	Cinquefoil
Foal's Foot	Tormentil
Frog's Foot	Club Moss
Goat's Beard	Coltsfoot
Goat's Foot	Bulbous Buttercups
Golden Star	Vegetable Oyster
Nose's Foot	Ash Weed
Hedgehogs	Avens
Honey Lotus	Clover
Horse Tail	Medicago Intertexta
Horse Tongue	Melilot
Hound's Tongue	Scouring Rush
Jew's Ear	Hart's Tongue
Joy of the Mountains	Vanilla Leaf
Lamb's Tongue	Fungus on Elder or Elm
Little Dragon	Marjoram
Lizard's Tail	Ribwort Plantain
Lizard's Tongue	Tarragon
Love...	Bress...

Contents

Acknowledgments

This book is also dedicated to others who supported my efforts: Darlene B., Mezdulene B., Barb A., Sara Camilli, Michelle V. C., Charles G., Glenn S., Harvey L., Judith J., Merren M., my nieces, nephews, and grandson serving in Kuwait. And to the many encouraging others.

— Sac...
n sm...
us —
an Go...
rasm...
derive
also
— Ma...
me
...
io...
...
Ble...
and atta...

...is burned in the
...of love when
...of Persephone,
...good healt...
...one is also God
...and trance stat...
...n the breasts t...
...See Orange Blos...
...nd third eye aid
...p.
...e cond...

—and cosmetic, internally and exter...
...young twigs are astringent, tonic, cleansing,
...ative.

...Sawdust. Can be used in many incenses. Woods have
...tary rulerships as the more expensive ingredients.
...e under the Moon and Venus; hard woods under Mars
..."redwoods" for Mars; expensive and rare woods for
...Jupiter; genuine Rosewoods under Venus; the "blackwoods"
...; walnut to the Sun; the commonly called "yellow-woods"
...and the Sun; "white or cream-woods," e.g. Ash, under the Moon.

...ruff (Asperula odorata)
...: Sweet Woodruff, Master of the Woods, Woodrove, Wuderove,
...Wuderope, Herb Walter
...t
...se
...Fire
...eities: Aries, Mars, Thor, Venus
...ed: The herb
...Powers: Purification
...ic Uses: Wonderfully fragrant; acquires its scent only as it
...Much used in perfumery and bath herb mixtures. An herb
...Spring, used to clear away the closeness and drab atmosphere
...e winter months. Carry when wishing to turn over a new leaf.
...to change your outlook in life, especially in the spring. Added
...the May Wine, the traditional witches' drink at Beltane. Brings
...tory to those who carry it.

Wormwood (Artemisia absinthium)
olk Names: Old Woman, Absinthe, Absinth, Crown for a King
...Hot
...times the Moon

...ovoyance, Protection
...ey magical herb sacred to the Moon
...cense on All Hallows Eve, and in charm
for... n, scrying, divination, prophecy, and a
...once burned in all incenses designed to raise spi...
...clairvoyance and divinatory incenses (especially
...with mugwort) as well as in exorcism and prot...
...onto fires on Samhain (Halloween) to gain protect...
...roaming the night. Burn while using a pendul...

Yarrow (Achillea millefolium)
Folk Names: Seven Year's Love, Sanguinary, Old M...
Herb, Old Man's Pepper, Soldier's Woundwort, T...
Nosebleed, Thousand Leaved, Hundred-Leaved Gr...
Arrow Root, Eerie, Ladies' Mantle, Knyghten, Ya...
Field Hops, Tansy, Gearwe, Noble Yarrow, Ya...
Devil's Plaything, Achillea, Snake's Grass
Gender: Cold
Planet: Venus
Element: Water
Assoc. Deities: Venus, Aphrodite, Hathor, Ir...
Parts Used: Flowers
Basic Powers: Love, Clairvoyance, Exorci...
Specific Uses: Used in divination spells
Sleeping with a bag of yarrow under o...
one's future spouse. Was a witches'...
and marriage charms, as it has the...
happily for 7 years. Worn as an am...
Held in the hand it stops all fea...
exorcism incenses. Considered a sac...
Chinese.
Yew (Taxus baccata)
Folk Names: Chinwood, English Yew
Gender: Cold
Planet: Saturn
Element: Earth

...n be
...wood is so...

Author's and Publisher's Note

The publisher and author are not responsible for the use and misuse of plants listed in this book, especially those labeled POISONOUS. With some of these plants, even touching can have negative effects. The plants are included with warnings in order to give a more complete study of herbs.

All plants, like all medicines, may be dangerous if used improperly or taken in excess or for too long a time. Be sure the herbs are fresh and know the strengths can vary.

We do not endorse or guarantee the curative effects of any of the subjects in this book.

...ed – gets its name from the Old Norse word "dill..."

...ragrant peppery scent reputed to...

...hen used with mint, citrus and...

...yptus – pungent, with a slight me...

...jpani – warm, rich, exotic oil.

...nia – heady, sweet fragrance is a...

...efruit – fresh, citrusy odor.

...rapin Crystals – ble... with cits...

...inth – fresh, tangy...

...ine – symbol of se...

...eductive scent; he...

...nd Oriental perfum...

...anum – heavy, s...

...from the resin of a...

...the Mediterrane...

...inds well with...

...nd musk. Also...

---

plants originally dedicated to the pagan goddesses... the common folk.

WICCAN NAME	COMMON NAME
Adder's Mouth	Stitch Wort
Adder's Meat	
Adder's Tongue	Dogstooth Violet
Ass' Ear	Comfrey
Bear's Ear	Auricula
Bear's Foot	Stinking Hellbore
Beehive	Snail Plant
Beggar's Tick	Cuckhold
Bird's Eye	False Hellebore
Bird's Tongue	European Ash
Black Dog Resin	Xanthorrhoea Arbor...
...dy's Fingers	Foxglove
	Marsh Marigold
	Coltsfoot
	Toadflax
	...owdrop

...and early July. British Herb Tobacco for relief of asthma and bronchitis; Coltsfoot predominantly, plus buckbean, eyebright, betony, rosemary, thyme, lavender, and chamomile.

Comfrey (Symphytum officinale)
Folk Names: Yalluc, Slippery Root, Boneset, Assear, Consolida, Healing Herb, Gum Plant, Consound, Bruisewort, Knitbone, Wallwort, Black Wort, Healing Blade, Salsify
Gender: Cold
Planet: Saturn
Element: Air
Assoc. Deities: Nephthys, Isis, Aemtes, Hecate
Parts Used: The herb, root
Basic Powers: Protection
Specific Uses: To ensure your safety while traveling carry some. Put in luggage to ensure its safety.

Copal Gum (Copalquahuitl)
Gender: Hot
Planet: Jupiter
Element: Fire/Water
Assoc. Deities: Jupiter, Zeus, Re, Osiris
Basic Powers: Prosperity
Specific Uses: Of Mexican origin, a fragrant, translucent white resin distilled from Copalquahuitl, Mexican Copalli incense. Originally found in Mexico, but is now found in Zanzibar, West Africa, Mozambique, Madagascar, and India.

Coriander (Coriandrum sativum)
Folk Names: Cilantro, Cilantro, Culantro, Chinese Parsley
Gender: Hot
Planet: Mars
Element: Fire
Assoc. Deities: Tiw, Horus
Parts Used: Seeds
Basic Powers: Love

...of Weights and Measures, their...

...d Apothecary Symbols and 6...
teaspoon
tablespoon
cup
cubic centimeter
= drachm or dram
dr = fluid drachm or dram
oz = fluid ounce
foot or feet
gram or grains

	SOLID	
	= 1/20 scruple	
...grains	= less than 1/8 teaspoon	= 5 drops or minims
grains	= 1/4 teaspoon	= 15 drops or minims
grains	= 1 scruple or 1/3 dram or 1/3 teasp.	= 20 drops or minims
grains	= 1 teaspoon or 1 dram + or 3 scruples	= 60 drops or minims or 1 fluidram
...ples	= 20 grains or 1/3 dram or 1/3 teasp.	= 20 drops or minims
	= 60 grains or 1 teasp. or 1 gram	= 60 drops or minims or 1 fluidram
...ight	= 24 grains or 1/20 ounce	= 24 drops or minim
	= 3 scruples or 1 teaspoon or 60 grains	= 60 drops or minims or 1 fluidram
	= 1/3 tablespoon or 1 dram or 60 grains or 5 grams or 3 scruples	= 60 drops or minims or 1 fluidram

---

...roma.

...es, violets

...

...ortality; sweet, herbaceous

...lary sage, lavender, rosem...

..."narkao" (to be stupified...

...egoism.

One

Introduction to Magical Folkhealing

What makes a person who they are is a very complicated question and path. Our personalities and lives are formed and affected by so many variables: karma, choices at each step in life, family experiences, genetics, the unexpected and/or unknowable…perhaps even astrology. No one can say for certain. Even within a family, very few members have totally the same personality or belief system. My father and my brother were, and are, very good dowsers, whether for water, water lines, or underground tanks. However, neither did (or do) believe in the same things as I do. For certain, we all are influenced more deeply by some people than by others.

Both sides of my family never considered themselves of any great importance. They were of very different types of personalities, which confused me but taught me many things. On my maternal grandparents' side were two brothers, James and Elijah John Smith, who married two sisters, Lily and Martha Green. James and Martha had nine children, while Elijah John and Lily had twelve. I was the oldest child in my parents' family of three and a girl with mostly male cousins, so it was a wild upbringing. The expression "fight or flight" comes to mind.

Both maternal grandparents died by the time I was seven years old. Although there were a few aunts and uncles who had the gift of premonition, they mostly chose to ignore it and dismissed it as fantasy for anyone who experienced it.

The paternal side didn't talk about their psychic experiences and folkhealing very much either. However, it was very quietly acknowledged within the family. My paternal grandmother, Clara Fern Long née Corbin, was the joy of my life after they moved from Iowa to Oregon when I was about three years old. She rarely refused to answer a question and encouraged me in my art, writing, and reading. Most importantly, she fed my soul and made me comfortable with the psychic.

I was full of questions, mostly about her family, and she answered them with patience and love. I learned that at one time we were a Southern family, which explained her expressions I find myself still using today. Her father, Richard Corbin, was Pennsylvania Dutch and Irish. Both sets of their parents moved south before the Civil War and were deep into folkhealing in Missouri. As a young man, Richard broke his arm badly while logging with his three brothers. His mother, Suzanne Deeds, set the arm as best she could, although it was always a little crooked. Knowing Richard and his stubbornness, it is likely he went back to logging too soon. He married Alice White, a healer and psychic who was Scots/Irish. After they lost five children in one winter to diphtheria, they moved to Iowa by means of a covered wagon with their two remaining children, one of them was my grandmother. After several miscarriages, Alice finally had two more children, Alice and Albert.

Alice White Corbin's father, Quincey, was a close friend with the local Native Americans and learned healing from them, passing on this information to his daughter. Being of Native American, Scots/Irish, and Pennsylvania Dutch descent, the gene pool was well stirred, churning out many psychics and folkhealers in every generation. The folkhealing was more than just treating the physical—it slid into areas of mental, emotional, and spiritual healing as well. By going to a conventional church regularly, they bypassed the stigma of being Pagan or nonbelievers, and their folkhealing was accepted because of the scarcity of good doctors.

I was born with a rare kidney disease which even Dorn-becker's Hospital in Portland, Oregon, could not diagnose or cure. My saving grace was a local Chinese herbalist who made me a tonic and pulled me back from death at less than a year old. I wish I knew the ingredients of that tonic today, as I still must live with chronic kidney disease.

One late autumn when I was about ten, I came down with a fever and some disease that put me in bed for two weeks with a headache that was the worst I've ever had, worse than a migraine. I couldn't tolerate to even have my hair brushed or turn my head; I couldn't eat and was in excruciating pain constantly. My grandmother, who had lived through the influenza epidemic of the 1920s, advised my mother to take me to the hospital, but my mother refused, saying I would "get over it." Grandmother had tended Granddad during the epidemic and knew there was little she could do. At that disastrous time they lived on the road to the local cemetery, and daily she and her two daughters watched the hearses go by in a nearly steady procession. Whatever she did with her healing helped Granddad get well, and the rest of the family escaped the disease. My grandfather lived to be ninety-two.

When I was ill, Grandmother did something she rarely did; she bypassed my mother and told my father her opin-ion. It deepened the division between the two women, but it saved my life. I couldn't eat, walk, talk above a whisper, or stand light or noise. The doctors decided it was a virus and kept me in the hospital for a week to ten days. While there, I ran into the problem of swallowing large pills, something that is still difficult for me to do. A kind nurse came up with a solution: the pill was put in a spoonful of jelly, which made the pill just slide on down. Gradually, I got well and grew even closer to my grandmother. However, the rift between her and my mother reached such a point that my grandmother never offered to heal again.

Throughout my teens and twenties, I carefully listened to what my grandmother said and did with herbs, flowers, and certain herbal scents. During this time, I wrote down what my grandmother said, in addition to what I learned about herbs, into various little notebooks. Finally, in my late twenties or early thirties, I faced the task of putting all these notebooks into one large book. It took a very long time. Even then, as I kept learning more, I put that information, line by cautious line, into the book. In the 1950s and 1960s, there were few reliable Pagan books on the market, especially in the backward areas in which I lived. Thus, many things were added helter-skelter at the end, not in the proper place. Fortunately, they were kept safe in the book, not destroyed or lost.

The book I chose was an innocuous type, with only a repeating bland floral pattern on the cover; nothing to catch anyone's eye or hint at its contents. This was necessary as the man I was married to at the time was a nonbeliever in everything and a harsh skeptic of herbs, their uses, and all things psychic. However, he always asked what I thought about his career changes and if they would further his desire to climb the social ladder. Two times I advised him not to invest in a venture and not to make a regional move. He did so anyway. Both times I was proved right; the last time was so disastrous it caused the dissolution of the marriage.

Around 2006, my good friend Dave happened to read the journal while visiting. He asked me why I had never submitted it for publication. I shrugged and answered that there are tons of herbals out there. Dave replied that he'd never seen one like mine. He commented that my journal went "beyond the physical and has more to do with the mental, emotional, and spiritual bodies."

After years of further contemplation, I thought perhaps it was time to submit it in hopes of publication.

Two

Tools Needed for Working with This Herbal

In our fantasies, we would have a separate room filled with tools and equipment mentioned by the ancient apothecaries. However, this isn't necessary—times have changed, and it is far easier to purchase small amounts of herbs and oils from reliable suppliers than it is to acquire tillable land, plant, grow, and harvest herbs, many of which can only be grown in special climates. The distillation of herbs into oils is a complicated process that requires a great amount of time, something most of us no longer have.

Whatever you decide to use as tools, it is best to keep them separate from your everyday household ones. A small ceramic or stone mortar and pestle can be used to powder herbs, as can a small electric coffee bean grinder. Just don't use the same grinder for both purposes; you don't want fragments of herbs tainting your coffee or vice versa. Intent concentration on the reasons for preparing the herbs is the same no matter the method you use.

The same principle of keeping your tools separate applies to the rest of your equipment: wooden stirring spoons, a small stainless steel bowl for blending, ground herbs, and any measuring spoons. If you plan to make a mixture large enough to least several times, you will need small glass containers with tight-fitting lids and labels for each container. Never fail to label jars—I guarantee you will not remember what you made and the quantities used at a later date.

Clean your herbal equipment carefully after each use. This ensures that there is no cross-contamination of purposes or contents when you use them again.

According to the traditions of Ireland and Scotland, using an iron kettle or equipment is an insult to the Fae, or fairy folk. However, this is according to ancient legends and may not apply to all the fairy folk any longer.

The most important—and least expensive—addition to your magickal equipment will be the power of your intent, purpose of will, and your belief that you can influence the matter for which you are working. Do not work spells to influence people. The only person you can change is your-self. Even if you influence someone for a short period of time to do or be what you want, they can easily repel that control, and the final outcome will be karma to pay. It is fine, however, to work for someone's health, financial problems, or protection. The depth of your concentration and determination during any mixing formula will determine how much power is put behind your desire. Reciting certain verses is a further verbal enhancement of that power, as is the burning of certain colored candles.

To fine-tune your power and intent, you may also want to time your efforts according to the moon phases (waxing moon is increasing, waning moon is decreasing), and the weekday ruled by a specific planet. The more specific things you use, do, say, and believe, the more you amplify your intent and purpose.

It is a good habit to copy ingredients of each spell you do, the time it took to manifest, and end results into your own magickal journal. In this way you can decide which ingredients might need to be changed, even how your intent and purpose may have affected the spell.

A warning about the uses of all herbs and oils: Unless you are well acquainted with an herb, such as peppermint, *never* ingest any herbs or oils unless you have been told it is safe to do so. Test for sensitivity or allergies to an herb or oil by rubbing the herb or putting a small drop of oil on the inside bend of your elbow. I discovered through touch that I am allergic to comfrey: each time I touched it, my hands got a rash; the final confirmation came when I used an herbal lip balm for chapped lips and got the same reaction: rough, blistered lips.

Do not burn herbs within an enclosed space or near anything flammable. Certain herbs cause nausea or mental disorientation when burned, and a few are deadly. Although listed in this book, some herbs should not be used or burned at all. They are in this book simply for their informational value.

In fact, it is much safer to burn herbs or candles inside a small cast-iron cauldron. Cast iron does not transfer much heat from the bottom, especially if it has small legs underneath. If still in doubt about safety, set the cauldron or metal bowl on another metal surface, such as a tray or the stove.

Three

Ancient Herbalists' and Apothecary Symbols

℔ Pound

ANA Equal amounts

℥ Ounce

ʒ Dram

P℥ Pinch

O℥ Pint

ℳ Still

Honey

Mix l

Boil

Э℥ Scruple

℞ Take

Distill

Filter

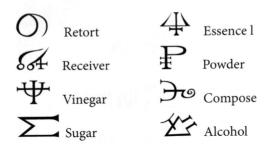

Although you may never run across these symbols, you may encounter them if you study some of the ancient books. The herbalists used this type of shorthand to avoid trouble with authorities of the time.

Four

Ancient Table of Weights and Measures

t = teaspoon
T = tablespoon
C = cup
cc = cubic centimeter
dr = drachm or dram
f 3 fl dr = fluid drachm or dram
f 3 fl oz = fluid ounce
' ft = foot or feet
g = gram or grains

g = gram or grains
" = one inch
M or min = minimum
oz = ounces
pt = pint
qt = quart
16 = pound
CS = scruple

	Solid	**Fluid**
Grain	= ¹⁄₂₀ of a scruple	
A few grains	= less than ⅛ teaspoon	= 5 drops or minims
15 grains		= 15 drops or minims
20 grains		= 20 drops or minims
60 grains or 1 dram or 3 scruples		= 60 drops or minims or 1 fluid dram
Scruple	= 20 grains or ⅓ dram or ⅓ teaspoon	= 20 drops or minims
3 scruples	= 60 grains or 1 teaspoon or 1 gram dram	= 60 drops or minim or 1 fluid
Pennyweight	= 24 grains or ¹⁄₂₀ ounce	= 24 drops or min v
Dram	= 3 scruples or 1 teaspoon or 60 grains	= 60 drops minims or 1 fluid ounce
Teaspoon	= ⅓ tablespoon or 1 dram or 60 grains or	= 60 drops or minims or 1 fluid drams .3 scruples
2 teaspoons	= 1 dessertspoon or 2 drams	= 120 drops or minims or 2 fluid drams
Tablespoon	= 3 teaspoons or 15 grams or ½ ounce	= 180 drops or minims or 15 cc or 3 fluid drams or ½ fluid ounce

	Solid	**Fluid**
2 tablespoons	= 30 grams or ⅛ cup 1 ounce or 8 drams	= 1 fluid ounce or 8 fluid drams or minims of 30 cc
4 tablespoons	= ¼ cup	= 2 fluid ounces or 60 cc
5⅓ tablespoons	= ⅓ cup	
Gill	= 8 tablespoons or ½ cup	= 4 fluid ounces or about 125 cc
2 gills	= 16 tablespoons or 1 cup or 8 ounces	= 8 fluid ounces or ½ pint
Ounce	= 16 drams (avoirdupois) or ⅛ cup	= 8 fluid drams
16 ounces	= 2 cups or 1 pint	= 128 fluid drams
32 ounces	= 1¾ pounds or 4 cups	= 32 fluid ounces or 2 pints or 1 quart
Pound	= 16 ounces (avoirdupois) or 12 ounces (troy)	
1 wineglass	= 3–4 tablespoons	= 1½–2 fluid ounces
1 teacup	= 8–10 tablespoons	= 4–5 fluid ounces

Apothecary's Weight

20 grains	= 1 scruple	= 20 grains
3 scruples	= 1 dram	= 60 grains
8 drams	= 1 ounce	= 480 grains
12 ounces	= 1 pound	= 5,760 grains

Avoirdupois Weight

274 grains	= 1 dram	= 27+ grains
16 drams	= 1 ounce	= 473+ grains
16 ounces	= 1 pound	= 7,000 grains

Fluid Measure

60 minims	= 1 fluid dram
8 drams	= 1 fluid ounce
20 ounces	= 1 pint
8 pints	= 1 gallon

These descriptions help when reading very old herbals or texts. If you want to keep your own herbal journal, you could use these measurements as a code. Just be certain you understand them.

Metric Conversions

US Volume Measure

¹⁄₁₆ teaspoon
⅛ teaspoon
¼ teaspoon
½ teaspoon
1 teaspoon
1 tablespoon (3 teaspoons)
2 tablespoons (1 fluid ounce)
⅛ cup (2 tablespoons)
¼ cup (4 tablespoons)
½ cup (4 fluid ounces)
1 cup (16 tablespoons)
1 pint (2 cups)
1 quart (4 cups)

Metric Equivalent

0.3 milliliter
0.5 milliliter
1.2 milliliters
5.0 milliliters
5.0 milliliters
14.8 milliliters
29.6 milliliters
29.6 milliliters
59.1 milliliters
118.3 milliliters
236.6 milliliters
473.2 milliliters
946.4 milliliters

US Volume Measure

¹⁄₁₆ ounce
⅛ ounce
¼ ounce
¾ ounce
1 ounce
1 ½ ounces
2 ounces
3 ounces
4 ounces
8 ounces

Metric Equivalent

1.8 grams
3.5 grams
7.0 grams
21.3 grams
28.3 grams
42.5 grams
56.7 grams
85.0 grams
113.4 grams
226.8 grams

US Volume Measure	Metric Equivalent
10 ounces	283.5 grams
12 ounces	340.2 grams
16 ounces	453.6 grams

Five

Folklore Names of Herbs, Flowers, and Trees

When old formulas began to be recorded, many early herbalists, magicians, and occultists wanted to keep the most powerful of the old magicks secret. So they used folklore names and symbolisms, and even added fanciful ingredients to the formulae.

The list of such names is quite long and varied, but here are a few examples: "bloody fingers" refers to foxglove. "Tongue of the dog" is simply hound's tongue, a common herb. "Blood" is the sap from an elder tree, and "eyes" refer to one of a group of plants resembling the eye, such as the aster, daisy, chamomile, or even eyebright. Crow's foot, dog's tooth, horse-tongue, and mouse-ear are all magickal, folklore, and dialectical names for herbs and plants.

Then, many plants were given folk names that revealed their uses in healing, magick, or the superstitions surrounding them. This is especially common in the British Isles where one plant can be known by as many as two dozen distinct names. Since almost all of the old herbal books came from Europe, you will find them cropping up again and again.

Finally, there are whole books of plants with appellations such as "Our Ladies Fingers" or "Old Man's Oatmeal." These are plants originally dedicated to the Pagan goddesses and gods of the common folk.

Folklore Name	Common Name
Adam and Eve	Lungwort
Adder's Mouth	Stitch Wort
Adder's Tongue	Dogstooth Violet
Albanum	Frankincense
Ass' Ear	Comfrey
Bear's Ear	Auricula
Bear's Foot	Stinking Hellebore
Beehive	Snail Plant
Beggar's Tick	Cuckhold
Bird's Eye	False Hellebore
Bird's Tongue	European Ash
Black Boy Resin	Xanthorrhoea Arbores

Folklore Name	Common Name
Bloody Fingers	Foxglove
Bull's Eyes Marsh	Marigold
Bull's Foot	Coltsfoot
Calf's Snout	Toadflax
Candlemas Maiden	Snowdrop
Candlewick Plant	Mullein
Catgut	Hoary Pea
Cat's Eye	Star Scabious
Cat's Foot	Canada Snake Root
Cat's Foot/Paw	Ground Ivy
Cat's Milk	Wartwort
Chicken Toe	Crawley Root
Cock's Comb	Yellow Rattle
Cow's Tail	Canada Fleabane
Crow Foot	Cranesbill
Crown for a King	Wormwood
Devil's Milk	Wartwort
Dew of the Sea	Rosemary
Dog's Tongue	Hound's Tongue
Donkey's Eyes	Cowage Plant
Dove's Foot	Cranesbill
Dragon's Claw	Crowley Root
Dragon's Eye	Nephalium Loganum
Dragonwort	Bistort
Duck's Foot	American Mandrake
Dwale	Deadly Nightshade
Earth Smoke	Fumitory

Folklore Name	Common Name
Elfwort	Elecampane
Enchanter's Plant	Vervain
Eye of the Star	Horehound
Fairy Fingers/Gloves	Foxglove
Five Finger Grass	Cinquefoil
Flesh and Blood	Tormentil
Foal's Foot	Coltsfoot
Fox Tail	Club Moss
Frog's Foot	Bulbous Buttercup
Garden Heliotrope	Valerian
Goat's Beard	Vegetable Oyster
Goat's Foot	Ash Weed
Golden Star	Avens
Hare's Foot	Clover
Hedgehogs	Medicago Intertexta
Honey Lotus	Melilot
Horse Tail	Scouring Rush
Horse Tongue	Hart's Tongue
Hound's Tongue	Vanilla Leaf
Jew's Ear	Fungus on Elder
Joy of the Mountains	Marjoram
Khus Khus	Vetavert
Lamb's Tongue	Ribwort Plantain
Little Dragon	Tarragon
Lizard's Tail	Breast Weed
Lizard's Tongue	Sauroglossum
Love-In-Idleness	Pansy

Folklore Name	Common Name
Love Parsley	Lovage
Loveroot	Orris Root
Low John	Galangal
Maiden's Ruin/Lad's Love	Southernwood
Master of the Woods	Woodruff
Masterwort	Angelica
May Lily	Lily of the Valley
Mistress of the Night	Shepherd's Purse
Moonlight on the Grove	Jasmine
Mother's Heart	Tuberose
Mouse Ear	Mouse Blood Wort
Mouse Tail	Common Stonecrop
Mugwort	French Lily
Negro's Head	Vegetable Ivory
Old Man's Beard	Fringe Tree
Ox Tongue	Bugloss
Password	Primrose
Queen of the Meadow	Meadowsweet
Rabbit's Foot	Field Clover
Ram's Head	American Valerian
Rat's Tail	Cat Tail
Ruddes	Marigold
Seven Year's Love	Yarrow
Shepherd's Heart	Shepherd's Purse
Sleep Wort	Lettuce
Snake Head	Balmony
Snake Milk	Blooming Spurge

Folklore Name	Common Name
Snake's Tongue	Adder's Tongue Fern
Sorcerer's Violet	Periwinkle
Squirrel Ear	White Plantain
Stag Horn	Club Moss
Starflower	Borage
Star of the Earth	Avens
Starweed	Chickweed
Starwort	Aster
Stinking Goose Foot	Chenopodium
Swine Snout	Dandelion
Thousand Seal	Yarrow
Thunder Plant	Houseleek
Toad	Toadflax
Unicorn Horn	True Unicorn Root
Wax Dolls	Fumitory
Witch Aspirin	White Willow Bark
Witch Bells	Foxglove
Witch Brier	Brier Hips
Witch Grass	Dog Grass
Witch Herb	Mugwort
Witch Wood	Rowan
Wolf's Claw	Lycopodium
Wolf's Foot	Bugle Weed

Six

Weekdays, Planets, and Zodiac Signs

Our modern weekdays are given rulership according to Roman deities. However, the actual names of several have a Viking origin. Sunday and Monday are self-explanatory: Sun's day and Moon's day. But Tuesday, ruled by Mars, was Tyr's Day; Wednesday, ruled by Mercury, was Wodan's Day; Thursday, ruled by Jupiter, was Thor's Day; and Friday, ruled by Venus, was Freyja's Day. Saturday was said to be ruled by Saturn.

In addition, each planet was believed to be more powerful during a certain hour of the day or night. Charts for the planetary symbols and daily hours are easily found online.

When reading the hour charts, always make adjustments for Daylight Saving Time. The idea behind using planetary days and hours is that you can connect with a stronger energy for use in spells. To use this system, decide which planet best symbolizes the type of spell you plan to do. Then select the proper day and hour in which to do your work.

The ancient herbals spoke of planets being masculine (hot) or feminine (cold). Masculine simply means diseases, situations, or problems that are hot, aggressive, or overly energetic. Feminine means cold, lack of energy, or more hidden in nature. Planets were also associated with an element —Earth, Air, Fire, or Water. The sun was considered masculine, hot, and with the element of Fire. The moon was feminine, cold, and of the element of Water. Mercury is the one planet of dual gender (asexual or bisexual), cold, and connected with Earth/Fire. Venus is a cold, feminine planet associated with Earth/Air. Mars is hot, masculine, and connects to Fire/Water. Jupiter also is hot, masculine, and goes with Fire/Water. Saturn changes the pattern slightly by being cold, masculine, and connected only to Earth.

Whether of folklore tradition or a magician, one should be aware of the powers said to be behind every planet. By learning which planet has the strongest powers of a certain type, you can fine-tune your work.

The Sun rules all operations involving employers, promotion, friendships, healing, divine powers, labor, and world leaders. It also rules plants with parts resembling it in shape and/or color, as the orange fruit, the reddish-orange spice saffron, and the flowers of chamomile, celandine, marigold, sunflowers, European angelica, lovage, rosemary, and rue. Other plants connected with the Sun are centaury, eyebright, storax, and walnuts. It is also connected with cinnamon, vanilla, laurel, heliotropin, olibanum. Heliotropin is a white crystalline powder, the solid form of the essential of the flower heliotrope or "cherry pie."

The Moon rules spells dealing with the home, family, agriculture, cooking, clairvoyance, medicine, dreams, and the sea. It also rules plants with parts similar in shape and/or color, such as bananas, mangos, melons, pumpkin, opium poppy, orris root, sweet flag, water lilies. Included in this connection are plants with high water content, often with soft, juicy leaves, such as cabbage, cucumber, lettuce, and plants that live in or near water: seaweed, watercress, willow, and wintergreen. The moon is also associated with camphor, galbanum (from a group of species in which cowparsely and angelica may also be found), almond, hazel, all lilies, bay, jasmine, and aromatic seeds.

Mercury, because of its airy nature, rules plants with fine, divided leaves, such as caraway, carrots, dill, fennel, and parsley, as well as medicinal plants that are related to the brain, nervous system, or organs of speech such as lavender, lily of the valley, marjoram, parsnip, elecampane, horehound, and the deadly mandrake.

Venus, as one would expect, rules plants with particularly pretty flowers, in her aspect as goddess of love and beauty; plants such as columbine, daisy, periwinkle, primrose, some roses, and violets. Her favorites among other fruits and plants are apple, blackberry, plum, raspberry, red cherries, red elderberry, strawberry, tomato. Others connected to this planet are birch, burdock, elder, feverfew, mother of thyme, sorrel tansy, thyme, and vervain.

Mars, as one would expect, rules plants with thorns or prickles, as the god of war and conflict; including barberry, cacti, hawthorn, and nettles. Mars also rules plants with strong, sharp, and spicy tastes: capers, coriander, garlic, gentian, hops, horseradish, mustards, peppers, radish, tobacco, wormwood, basil, sarsaparilla, and tarragon. It also rules opoponax, aloeswood, and dragon's blood resin. Do not use Barabados aloe or Cape aloe in incense, as their smell is quite unpleasant. When the aloes of the rare Liliaceae of Socotra Island is called for, use eagle-wood or find a substitute.

Jupiter rules over certain nutritious fruits and nuts, such as almond, chestnut, currant, fig, olive, rose hips; this planet is also historically linked to the oak tree. Juniper is associated with plants with a pleasant scent: anise, balm, cloves, English myrrh, jasmine, linden, meadowsweet, and nutmeg, as well as chervil, cinquefoil, dandelion, docks, sage, mulberry, and the fir tree. Other plants under Jupiter's influence are nutmeg, cedar wood, and cedar's oil.

Saturn is a planet of rings and therefore rules over shrubs or trees that show annual growth rings such as elm, cypress, and pine. It also rules plants with cooling qualities such as barley, comfrey root, and tamarind. It rules over poisonous or narcotic plants, although I do not recommend using them: hellebore, hemlock, monkshood, yew, mezercon, and marijuana. It is safer to use quince, red beets, sloe, and Solomon's seal, or others that correspond such as myrrh, asafetida, violet leaves, Lignum Vitae, poppy, or oil of violet.

Plants and Signs of the Zodiac

A plant can be ruled by both a planet or the sun or moon and a sign of the zodiac. It is your mental and emotional intent of the spell that determines the outcome. By the time of the later herbals, the planets of Uranus and Neptune were included, but only in the use of the zodiac signs.

Aries. Masculine; the planet Mars. Affects the head and face. This sign rules over many of the same plants ruled by Mars, including cacti, garlic, hops, mustard, nettle, onion, peppers, radish; others are betony, lichens, and rosemary.

Taurus. Feminine, the planet Venus. Affects the throat and neck. Rules over many planets of Venus, plus lovage and plants of the earth, such as mushrooms.

Gemini. Masculine, the planet Mercury. Affects the hands, arms, shoulders, collarbone, lungs, and nervous system. It rules mosses because it is an airy sign, but also tansy and vervain.

Cancer. Feminine, the Moon. Affects the breast and stomach. It rules many plants ruled by the Moon, as both Cancer and the Moon relate to water. Plants are cucumber, lettuce, melons, rushes, water lilies, agrimony, alder, lemon balm, honeysuckle, hyssop, jasmine.

Leo. Masculine, the Sun. Affects the heart, sides, and upper portion of the back. It rules over many of the same plants as the Sun, and also over chamomile, celandine, European angelica, eyebright, marigold, orange, rue, saffron, borage, bugloss, peony, and poppy.

Virgo. Feminine, the planet Mercury. Affects the solar plexus and bowels. This zodiac sign is dedicated to Ceres, the Roman goddess of agriculture and thus rules cereal plants: oats, barley, rye, wheat, grasses, and sedges.

Libra. Masculine, the planet Venus. Affects the kidneys, loin area, ovaries, lower portion of the back. Rules many of the same plants as Venus: apple, cherry, primrose, strawberry, white rose, and violet.

Scorpio. Feminine, the planet Mars. Affects the bladder and the sex organs. As the ruler of the sex organs, Scorpio governs plants that could be considered phallic symbols such as palms as well as flowers like calla lilies. It also governs basil, bramble, and wormwood.

Sagittarius. Masculine, the planet Jupiter. Affects the liver, hips, thighs, and the condition of the blood. As the centaur and ruler of the forests, Sagittarius governs forest trees and catkins. Associated with oak, beech, elm, all the mallows and feverfew.

Capricorn. Feminine, the planet Saturn. Affects the knees and spleen. Rules over comfrey cypress, hemlock, nightshades, yew, all plants that are also governed by Saturn.

Aquarius. Masculine, the planet Uranus. Affects the calves, ankles, and distribution of body fluids. Rules frankincense and myrrh.

Pisces. Feminine, the planet Neptune. Rules over algae, seaweed, and water mosses.

The Magick of Trees

Various trees were associated with the planets: the **Sun** with the bay, palm, walnut, ash, and the citrus family; the **Moon** with willow, ash, and trees abundant with sap or having an affinity with water; **Mars** with the pine and hawthorn, trees that are prickly and thorny; **Mercury** with nut-bearing trees (not necessarily edible), myrtle, pomegranate, hazelnut, mulberry; **Jupiter** with birch, vines, fig, oak, olive, lime, maple, and fir; **Venus** with apple, fig, elder, plum, peach, alder, birch, pear, and sycamore; **Saturn** with pine, yew, elm, beech, cypress, ivy, poplar, and quince.

The wood of sacred trees was used in ritual fires and to make magick wands of power. Sabbath need-fires were traditionally made of nine woods: oak, ash, cherry, rowan, birch, holly, hawthorn, fir, and pine. Elder and willow were not burned, for it might result in very bad luck. A special fire for visions and pyromancy was called the Fire of Azrael and was composed of juniper, cedar, and sandalwood.

Magick wands for various purposes were made from the branches of sacred trees. Willow wands were for Moon magick and divining for water, and hazel and hawthorn for general magick. The wood of sacred trees was also used for pentacles, knife handles, talismans, altars, statues, and other ritual objects. Branches, leaves, and flowers were also used as circle and temple decorations. Because it was believed that dryads and other spirits lived in many trees, it was important to ask permission before cutting or picking parts of trees. Permission was granted by the trees' behavior. If the tree remained silent, permission was granted. However, if there was any sudden stirring of the branches or trembling of the leaves, permission was not granted. If one cut without permission, one would raise the ire of its fairy, dryad, or sprite, and bad luck would come the person's way.

The ancient Celts developed an entire symbolic system, where sacred trees were associated with months and sabbaths or holy days; it was an alphabet of birds, stones, colors, and a secret Druidic system of sign language. The seven trees of the sacred Irish groves were alder, birch, willow, holly, hazel, oak, and apple.

Celtic Trees and Months

Beith	December 24–January 20	Birch
Luis	January 21–February 17	Rowan
Nion	February 18–March 17	Ash
Fearn	March 18–April 14	Alder
Saille	April 15–May 12	Willow
Uath	May 13–June 9	Hawthorn
Duir	June 10–July 7	Oak
Tinne	July 8–August 4	Holly or holly oak
Coll	August 5–September 1	Hazel
Muin	September 2–September 29	Vine
Gort	September 30–October 27	Ivy
Peith or Ngetal	October 28–November 24	Dwarf Elder or reed
Ruis	November 25–December 23	Elder

The Celtic Holy Days

Ailm	December 24	Silver Fir
Onn	Spring Equinox	Furze
Ur	Summer Solstice	Heather
Eadha	Autumn Equinox	Aspen
Idho	Winter Solstice	Yew
Oll-iach	December 23	Mistletoe

Seven

Herbs and Trees for Magick and Well-Being

The "gender" of an herb refers to the type of energy the plant emits. If a plant's influence is stimulating, aggressive, electric, and/or positive, it is considered to be "hot" or masculine. Plants that are relaxing, passive, magnetic and/or negative are considered "cold" or feminine.

The Latin and folk names are given to help distinguish one herb from another, as many have similar names but quite different properties.

The listed deities are not the only deities associated with each plant. Each pantheon around the world has similar gods or goddesses who are suitable to call upon when using a plant.

Sometimes, not all categories of an herb are given, as they do not apply or are unavailable.

Sachet bags are small bags that contain scented magickal herbs; these are usually carried on the body. The herbs should be ground fine for this use. A charm bag is another small bag of ground herbs that also has a small charm, such as a good luck charm: metallic four-leaf clover, a word of power, or a slip of paper to remind yourself what the charm is for. It can be worn or carried in a pocket. Potpourris are different: the herbs, flower petals, and spices do not need to be ground. They usually have a few drops of appropriate scented oils added, and are kept in an open bowl. I have an old potpourri jar that has a lid with holes in it.

Absinthe: *See Wormwood.*

Acacia (*Acacia senegal*)

Gender: Hot

Planet: Sun

Element: Air

Associated Deities: Osiris, Astarte, Ishtar, Diana

Parts Used: Twigs, wood, gum

Basic Powers: Protection, clairvoyance

Specific Uses: Burn with sandalwood during meditation to seek illumination and to develop the psychic powers.

Carry the wood as a protective amulet.

A thick paste of its sawdust or ground twigs can be mixed with aromatic herbs and oils, and shaped into scented beads. Use a thick, long needle to make a hole for stringing before you set the beads to dry. Acacia flowers (sweet acacia or mimosa) are used in perfumery and burned as an offertory incense to a goddess during love rituals or added to psychic vision incense.

Aconite (*Aconitum napellus*)

Folk Names: Wolf's Bane, Leopard's Bane, Monk's Hood

Gender: Cold

Planet: Saturn

Element: Earth

Associated Deities: Hecate, Cerridwen

Part Used: Herb. (POISONOUS)

Basic Powers: Knowledge, binding

Special Uses: Not recommended

Adam and Eve Root: *See Lungwort.*

Alder (*Alnus glutinosa*)

Gender: Hot

Planet: Mars

Element: Fire

Associated Deities: Astarte, Bran the Blessed

Parts Used: Inner bark, leaves, flowers, wood

Basic Powers: Divination, spells

Specific Uses: Whistles from green alder branches were made for whistling up the wind; they can also be made into panpipes. The twigs were used in ritual fires. The alder yields three dyes: red from the bark, green from the flowers (which is said to be the dye used by the fairies), and brown from the twigs.

Allspice (*Pimento officinalis*)

Folk Names: Clove pepper, Jamaica pepper, pimento

Gender: Hot

Planet: Mars

Element: Fire

Associated Deities: Horus, Mars, Tiw

Parts Used: Immature fruit, particularly the shell or rind

Basic Powers: Protection, energy

Specific Uses: Used for fragrance in perfumery and potpourris. It smells like a combination of cloves, juniper berries, cinnamon, and pepper.

Almond (*Amygdalus communis*)

Folk Names: Sweet almond, bitter almond, Greek nuts, Jordan almond

Gender: Hot

Planets: Sun, sometimes Venus

Element: Fire

Associated Deities: Horus, Ra, Apollo, Adonis, Lugh, Bel, Bast, Sekhmet

Parts Used: Flower, nut, oil, wood, kernels

Basic Power: Prosperity

Specific Uses: It can be used to make wands for general magick. Sweet almond oil can be used as a base for herbal oils and creams. The flower is the symbol of true love inextinguishable by death.

Aloe, Lignum (*Aquilaria agallocha*)

Gender: Cold

Planet: Venus

Element: Water

Associated Deities: Jupiter, Venus

Part Used: Wood

Basic Power: Love

Specific Uses: Resinous wood greatly esteemed as incense and also put into potpourris and sachets. Especially used in Jupiter and Venus incenses. Along with musk and myrtle it can be used as a burnt offering to the Goddess.

Amanita (*Amanita phalloides, Amanita muscaria*)

  Folk Names: Death Angel, Death Cap; Fly Agaric

  Gender: Cold

  Planet: Saturn

  Element: Earth

  Associated Deities: Nephthys, Isis, Hecate,
    Cerridwen, Saturn

  Part Used: The fungus. (POISONOUS)

  Basic Powers: Visions, prophecy

  Specific Uses: The Death Angel mushroom is a white,
    deadly, very poisonous fungus. *A. Muscaria* (fly
    agaric) is hallucinogenic and still poisonous, but a
    little less than *A. phalloides*. Fly agaric is the *soma*
    spoken of in the legends of Europe and Siberia,
    the vision and ecstasy produced by the sacred
    mushroom used by shamans and special spiritual
    leaders. I do not recommend its usage at all.

Ambergris

  Gender: Hot

  Planet: Venus

  Element: Air/Earth

  Associated Deities: Aphrodite, Astarte, Freyja, Hathor

  Parts Used: Total substance; comes from whales

Basic Power: Love

Special Uses: Fatty substance that resembles wax and is found in the intestines and stomach of the sperm whale. Synthetic ambergris should be used. It is used in perfumery as a fixative.

Anemone (*Anemone pulsatilla*)

Folk Names: Windflower, Pasque flower

Gender: Hot

Planet: Mars

Element: Fire

Associated Deities: Adonis, Venus

Part Used: Flowers

Basic Power: Healing

Specific Uses: Healing charms and amulets. Gather a perfect bloom when the first flowers appear in the spring; tie up in a red cloth, and carry as a guard against disease.

Angelica (*Angelica archangelica* or *A. officinalis, umbrelliferae*)

Folk Names: Masterwort, archangel, garden angelica

Gender: Hot

Planet: Sun

Element: Fire

Associated Deities: Venus

Parts Used: Leaves, root, seeds

Basic Powers: Protection, Exorcism

Specific Uses: Grow in your garden as a protection.
Carry the root with you as an amulet. Burn the dried
leaves in exorcism rituals. Said to protect against evil
spells and enchantment, the herb is said to be sacred
to the Archangel Michael. Also considered sacred
in China, where it is believed to guard against evil
spirits, spells, and enchantments. This herb produces
a resinous gum much like the fixative benzoin, and it
is often as a substitute for benzoin in perfumes.

Anise (*Pimpinella anisum*)

Folk Names: Anneys, Aniseed

Gender: Hot

Planet: Jupiter, sometimes Mercury

Element: Air

Associated Deities: Jupiter, Zeus, Mercury, Hermes

Part Used: Seeds

Basic Powers: Protection, purification

Specific Used: The seed averts the evil eye. A good
general cleansing spiritual bath is made with a
handful of anise seeds and a few bay leaves. This
is especially effective if you have accidentally or

unintentionally killed something. Under a pillow, anise seeds keep away nightmares.

Apple (*Pyrus malus*)

Folk Names: Fruit of the Underworld, Silver Bough, Tree of Love, Silver Branch

Gender: Cold

Planet: Venus

Element: Water

Associated Deities: Venus, Hercules, Diana, Dionysus, Olwen, Apollo, Hera, Athena

Parts Used: Fruit, juice, blossoms

Basic Powers: Love, healing, binding

Specific Uses: Add apple blossoms to love and healing incenses. Cut an apple into three pieces; rub each on a sick person's body and then bury the apple. The decaying apple is said to cure the illness. The same ritual can be done with warts. Use apple cider in place of blood or wine if either are called for in old magickal spells and rites. It is traditional to eat an apple on Samhain (Halloween); also cut an apple in half crossways to reveal a five-point star. Apples are sometimes used in place of a poppet in a spell.

Arbutus (*Arbutus unede*)

Folk Name: Strawberry tree

Gender: Cold

Planet: Moon

Element: Water

Associated Deities: Isis, Khensu, Neith, Diana, Luna, Morrigan

Part Used: Berries

Basic Power: Divination

Specific Uses: At one time in Ireland, where this shrub grows profusely, the berries were eaten or made into a narcotic wine for visions and prophecy.

Aromatic Rush: *See Calamus.*

Artemisia: *See Mugwort.*

Asafoetida (*Ferula foetida*)

Folk Names: Devil's dung, food of the gods

Gender: Hot

Planet: Saturn

Element: Fire

Associated Deities: Saturn, Kronos, Mars, Thor, Odin

Part Used: Herb

Basic Powers: Exorcism, purification

Specific Uses: A very vile-smelling root whose resin is quite agreeable in combination with other perfumes. Used as incense, it is believed to drive away evil spirits. When worn around the neck, it wards off disease. It is one of the ingredients in Voodoo "Ouanga" powder.

Ash (*Fraxinus excelsior* or *F. Americana*)

Folk Name: Nion

Gender: Hot

Planet: Sun

Element: Water

Associated Deities: Poseidon, Odin, Thor, Mars, Gwydion, Neptune

Parts Used: Leaves, branches

Basic Powers: Protection, prophecy, healing

Specific Uses: The ash spirits are called the Meliai, who give inspiration. The tree itself symbolizes rebirth. Druidic wands were fashioned of ash with spiral decorations carved into them. Ash wands are good for general magick, and especially solar magick and healing. In the Druidic tradition, ash is ruled by the Sun and the leaves were used in a ritual where they were scattered in the four directions accompanied by an invocation to the forces of life (for purposes of wealth, success, healing, and other matters ruled by the Sun). The fresh leaves are said to induce prophetic dreams if placed under one's pillow. Carve some of the wood into an equal-armed cross as a protection against drowning. The traditional witch's broom is made from an ash staff, together with birch twigs and a willow binding. Magick healing wands are often made from ash branches. If mandrake root is not available, poppets are often carved of ash roots to be used in healing and other rituals. Use in sea rituals of all kinds.

Aspen (*Populus tremula* in Europe; *Populus tremuloides* in America)

Folk Names: White Popular, Quaking Aspen

Gender: Cold

Planet: Saturn

Element: Earth

Associated Deities: The Great White Goddess, any powerful goddesses

Parts Used: Bark, wood

Basic Powers: Knowledge, reincarnation, overcoming curses

Specific Uses: This is a tree of old age and resurrection, and it rules the Autumn Equinox. In ancient times, shields were made of its wood.

Aster (*Aster* spp.)

Folk Name: Michaelmas Daisy

Gender: Hot

Planet: Venus

Element: Earth/Air

Associated Deities: Aphrodite, Astarte, Freyja, Brigid

Parts Used: Leaves, flowers

Basic Power: Love

Specific Uses: The leave and flowers are used to decorate the Autumn Equinox altar in the Druidic tradition.

Avens (*Geum urbanum*)

Folk Names: Herb Bennet, Star of the Earth, Yellow Avens, Blessed Herb, Golden Star

Gender: Hot

Planet: Jupiter

Element: Fire

Associated Deities: Amun, Zeus, Jupiter, Ptah, Odin, Indra, Vishnu

Part Used: Herb

Basic Power: Protection

Specific Uses: The herb and root, dug on March 25 to be its most powerful, was used as a spring tonic and blood purifier. Carry as an amulet to guard against wild animals and evil spirits. Burn during exorcisms and cleansing rituals. Add to protective sachets, amulets, and incenses.

Balm (*Melissa officinalis*)

Folk Names: Sweet Balm, lemon balm, Melissa

Gender: Hot

Planet: Jupiter

Element: Fire/Water

Associated Deities: Zeus, Amun, Don, the Dagda

Part Used: Herb

Basic Powers: Love, luck

Specific Uses: It is used in love charms and potion. Used in the bath, it is said to help with melancholy or depression.

Balm of Gilead (*Populus candicans, Commiphora opobalsamum*)

Folk Names: Balm of Mecca, Balsam of Gilead, Mecca Balsam, poplar, black poplar. In the South, black poplar buds are known as gilly or gilliam buds.

Gender: Cold

Planet: Saturn

Element: Earth

Associated Deities: Cerridwen, Isis, Nephthys, Hecate

Part Used: Buds

Basic Powers: Protection, intellect, manifestations, healing

Specific Uses: The resinous juice of this tree is very rare and has many strange mystical associations. In this country, Balm of Gilead or Buds of Gilead (*Populus Candicans, P. nigra,* or *P. balsmifera*) are poplar buds and are used in incense and perfumery. They are steeped in wine to make a love potion. Added to love sachets, they are carried on the person to mend a broken heart and protect from evil. Burn to set up a material basis in which spirits may manifest during ceremonies of this kind. An old Southern recipe for arthritis is to gently simmer a handful of gilly buds in a pint of light olive or sweet almond oil in a pan with a lid; strain out the buds and store the liquid in a dark colored bottle with a tight lid. Massage a small amount at a time gently into the arthritic joints, making certain you do not over-oil. *See also Poplar.*

Balsam of Peru (*Myroxylon pereirae*)

Folk Name: Toluifera Pereira

Gender: Hot

Planet: Sun

Element: Fire

Associated Deities: Horus, Ra, Apollo, Bast, Sekhmet,
 Lugh, Bel, Adonis

Part Used: Resin

Basic Powers: Success, control

Specific Use: Has a warm aromatic scent when burned
 as incense in success spells.

Balsam of Tolu (*Myrospermum toluiferum*)

Folk Name: Balsamum Americanum

Gender: Hot

Planet: Sun

Element: Fire

Associated Deities: Horus, Ra, Apollo, Bast, Sekhmet,
 Lugh, Bel, Adonis

Part Used: Liquid resin

Basic Powers: Success, control

Specific Uses: Either mix with other herbs or rub on
 candles when doing spells for success. It has a sweet,
 aromatic odor resembling vanilla or benzoin when
 burned.

Basil (*Ocimum basilicum*)

Folk Names: American Dittany, Alabahac, Sweet Basil,
 Witches' Herb, Our Herb

Gender: Hot

Planet: Mars

Element: Fire

Associated Deities: Krishna, Vishnu

Parts Used: Herb

Basic Powers: Purification, protection, exorcism, love

Specific Uses: Add to exorcism and protection incenses. It can be used as an ingredient of purification bath sachets. Often used in wealth and prosperity rituals. Add to love sachets and incenses. When basil leaves are strewn, burned, or grown, evil will not abide. It also helps with fertility of projects as well as human desires.

Bay Laurel (*Laurus nobilis*)

Folk Names: Bay, Bay Tree, Grecian laurel, Indian bay, Roman laurel, Sweet, Baie

Gender: Hot

Planet: Sun

Element: Fire

Associated Deities: Aesclepius, Apollo, Ceres, Cerridwen

Part Used: Leaves

Basic Powers: Protection, clairvoyance, exorcism, purification, healing

Specific Uses: Burn the leaves to induce visions. Wear
as an amulet to ward off negativity and evil. Burn
while smudging the house rooms in exorcism and
purification rituals. Put the leaves under the pillow
to induce inspiration and prophetic dreams. Add to
purification incenses and baths. Also add to healing
incenses and sachets. Traditionally, one should pick
the leaves while facing east, just at sunrise. Said to
offer protection against lightning. *See also Laurel.*

Bayberry (*Myrica cerifera*)

Folk Names: Wax myrtle, candleberry, tallow shrub

Gender: Hot

Planet: Jupiter

Element: Fire/Water

Associated Deities: Jupiter, Zeus, Amun, Isis

Parts Used: Dried bark of the root; the wax

Basic Power: Healing

Specific Uses: A synonym for the wild cinnamon of
the West Indies and South America, which yields
bay rum. In large doses it is emetic. Decoction of
the bark can be used as a gargle for chronic throat
inflammation.

Bdellium (*Commiphora* spp.)

Gender: Hot

Planet: Mars

Element: Fire

Associated Deities: Tiw, Thor, Horus

Parts Used: Gum resin

Basic Powers: Protection, conflict

Specific Uses: Similar to myrrh and balm of Gilead. It was used in ancient India in potions and charms against disease.

Beech (*Fagus sylvatica*)

Gender: Cold

Planet: Mercury

Element: Earth/Air

Associated Deities: Hermes, Thoth, Anubis, Maat, Odin

Parts Used: Wood, tar, oil of the nuts

Basic Power: Prophecy

Specific Uses: An old symbol for writing and literature; ancient runic tablets were made from it. The Franks used the tree as an oracle by listening to the wind through the leaves.

Belladonna (*Atropa belladonna*)

Folk Names: Deadly nightshade, dwale, banewort

Gender: Cold

Planet: Saturn

Element: Earth

Associated Deities: Hecate, Cerridwen, Kronos

Parts Used: The entire herb is POISONOUS.

Basic Powers: Knowledge, binding, hexes

Specific Uses: Although it was once used to induce astral projection and visions, I do NOT recommend using this plant for anything. It was always picked May Eve and was a common ingredient in flying ointments. In ancient times it was sometimes used to deaden the pain of a hard childbirth and the pain of burning during the Burning Times. A bit of this herb was secretly slipped to the condemned man or woman on his/her way to the pyre or scaffold. Quickly swallowed, the herb helped the accused drowse her way to the Otherworld.

Benzoin (*Styrax benzoin*)

Folk Names: Benjamen, gum benzoin, Siam benzoin

Gender: Hot

Planet: Sun

Element: Air

Associated Deities: Bast, Sekhmet, Osiris, Horus, Odin, Apollo

Part Used: Gum

Basic Powers: Intellectual, purification

Specific Uses: Burn with cinnamon for business success. Use in purification incenses to clear the surrounding area. A tincture of benzoin is used to preserve magickal oils. Burn during incantation at séances.

Bergamot, Wild (*Monarda didyma, M. fistulosa*)

Folk Names: Bee Balm, Oswego Tea, horsemint, Monarda

Gender: Hot

Planet: Jupiter

Element: Fire/Water

Associated Deities: Jupiter, Zeus, Amun

Parts Used: Leaves, flowers

Basic Powers: Friendships, health

Specific Uses: Used in sachets and incense. It also makes a good herbal tea, with a slightly spicy, orange-like flavor. The scent of this herb gives Earl Grey tea its distinct flavor.

Bethroot (*Trillium pendulum, trillium erectum*)

Folk Names: John the Conqueror, wake robin, Southern John, lamb's quarters, Indian shamrock

Gender: Hot

Planet: Sun

Element: Fire

Associated Deities: Horus, Ra, Apollo, Bast, Sekhmet, Lugh, Bel, Adonis

Part Used: Root

Basic Uses: Success, prosperity, luck

Specific Use: A piece of root is carried as a charm to draw success in all things.

Betony (*Stachys officinalis, Betonica officinalis, Stachys betonia*)

Folk Names: Bishopwort, lousewort, wood betony, purple betony

Gender: Hot

Planet: Jupiter

Element: Fire

Associated Deities: Zeus, Amun, the Dagda

Part Used: The herb

Basic Powers: Protection, purification

Specific Uses: A very magickal herb for Druids. It was said to have power against evil spirits, fearful visions, nightmares, and despair wherever it was carried, hung, or strewn in the house. It makes a protective wall when sprinkled near all doors and windows. A betony sleep pillow keeps away bad dreams. Add to all incenses of purification and protection. Burn in outdoor fires and jump through the cleansing smoke, especially at the Summer Solstice.

Birch (*Betula alba*)

Folk Names: White birch, canoe birch, paper birch, Lady of the Woods, mountain mahogany

Gender: Cold

Planet: Venus

Element: Earth/Air

Associated Deities: Venus, Aphrodite, Astarte, Hathor, Freyja, Brigid

Parts Used: Bark, leaves, wood

Basic Powers: Love, protection

Specific Uses: This is the tree of conception and birth. If a spirit appears wearing or carrying birch leaves and branches, it is the sign of a benevolent spirit. Birch has the power to keep away evil spirits which is why it was often used to make cradles. It represents solar energy and is the divinatory tree for matters of love. In the northern latitudes, the sacred soma, or *Amanita muscaria*, often grows under this tree. Birch oil has the characteristic odor of Russian leather.

Bistort (*Polygonum bistorta*)

Folk Names: Patience dock, snakeweed, dragonwort, sweet dock, osterick, passions, English serpentary, red legs, Easter giant

Gender: Cold

Planet: Saturn

Element: Earth

Associated Deities: Apollo, Gwydion, Thoth, Merlin, Isis, Cerridwen, Selena

Parts Used: The herb, or dried root gathered in March

Basic Powers: Clairvoyance, fertility

Specific Uses: An herb of psychics, it is used in divination incenses, especially with frankincense. Carry some with you if you wish to conceive.

Bittersweet (*Solanum dulcamara*)

Folk Name: Woody nightshade

Gender: Cold

Planet: Saturn

Element: Earth

Associated Deities: Circe, Hecate

Parts Used: Leaves, twigs. POISONOUS.

Basic Powers: Protection, overcoming obstacles

Specific Uses: One of Circe's favorite herbs. It can be placed under one's pillow to forget a lost love.

Blackberry (*Rubus fruticosus*)

Planet: Venus

Parts Used: Leaves, berries

Specific Uses: The leaves in tea or jelly are used for dysentery and diarrhea. Use as an infusion for stomach disorders. The tea can also be used as a gargle for sore throats and gum inflammations.

Blackthorn (*Prunus spinosa*)

Folk Names: Sloe, Mother of the Wood

Gender: Hot

Planet: Mars

Element: Fire

Associated Deities: Sekhmet, Nephthys, Anubis, Hecate, Pluto, Nudd, Morrigan

Parts Used: Wood, thorns

Basic Powers: Hexing, black magick

Specific Uses: The tree or bush is connected with black magick and blasting spells. The thorns can be used for sticking into wax images of one's enemies. The wands of this wood are frequently made into sturdy walking stick, thus keeping ill will away.

Bloodroot (*Sanguinaria canadensis*)

Folk Names: Indian Paint, Tetterwort, Red Root

Gender: Cold

Planet: Saturn

Element: Earth

Associated Deities: Kronos, Saturn, Hecate, Cerridwen

Part Used: The herb. POISONOUS.

Basic Powers: Protection, overcoming curses.

Specific Use: Sprinkle around a building to ward off evil.

Bog Asphodel (*Narthecium ossifragum* or *N. californicum*)

Gender: Cold

Planet: Saturn

Element: Earth

Associated Deities: Persephone

Part Used: Roots. POISONOUS.

Basic Powers: Overcoming curses, protection.

Specific Uses: Sacred to Persephone and the Underworld, it was said this herb protected one from sorcery.

Boldo (*Peumus boldus*)

Folk Names: Boldu, Boldoa fragrans

Gender: Hot

Planet: Mars

Element: Fire

Associated Deities: Tiw, Aries, Mars

Part Used: Leaves

Basic Power: Protection

Specific Uses. Leaves of this plant were placed at the four quarters of a dwelling to protect it from black magick.

Boneset (*Eupatorium perfoliatum*)

Folk Names: Thoroughwort, agueweed, teasel, feverwort, Indian sage

Gender: Cold

Planet: Saturn

Element: Earth

Associated Deities: Ceres, Cerridwen, Hecate

Part Used: Herb

Basic Power: Binding

Specific Uses: Often used to stuff poppets and voodoo dolls

Borage (*Borago officinalis*)

Folk Names: Nepenthe, burrage, bugloss, bee bread

Gender: Hot

Planet: Jupiter

Elements: Fire/Water

Associated Deities: Zeus, Jupiter, the Dagda

Parts Used: Leaves, flowers

Basic Powers: Health, the heart's desires

Specific Uses: This is the famous Nepenthe of Homer that would cause forgetfulness. It is mixed with mugwort and parsley to increase clairvoyance. This herb has been used for at least four hundred years for melancholy or minor depression.

Bramble (*Rubus fruticosus* or *R. villosus*)

Folk Names: Blackberry, dewberry, thimbleberry,
cloudberry

Gender: Cold

Planet: Venus

Element: Earth/Air

Associated Deities: The Great Goddess, Astarte, Freyja,
Hathor

Parts Used: Leaves, fruit

Basic Powers: Creativity, love

Specific Uses: Sacred to the Goddess in general,
as are other plants with five-pointed leaves. Five
is symbolic of the Goddess as She rules birth,
initiation, love, repose, and death.

Briar (*Rosa rubiginosa* or *R. canina*)

Folk Names: Briar Rose, sweet briat, eglantine, dog
rose, hip fruit, wild brier, witches' brier

Gender: Hot

Planet: Jupiter

Element: Fire/Water

Associated Deities: The Great Goddess, Zeus, Amun,
the Dagda, Thor

Parts Used: Flowers, fruit

Basic Powers: Luck, honor, richness

Specific Uses: This plant has highly odorous leaves, especially just after a shower. It symbolizes beauty and attainment in the midst of adversity and suffering. This has basically the same properties and uses as other roses.

Broom (*Cytisus scoparius*)

Folk Names: Link, genista, banal, Scotch broom, Irish broom

Gender: Hot

Planet: Mars

Element: Air

Associated Deities: Thor, Mars, Isis, Hecate, Cerridwen, Morrigan, Apollo

Part Used: Herb

Basic Powers: Purification, protection, wind spells

Specific Uses: The Druids considered this shrub to be a tree. It can be substituted for furze as the ruler of the Spring Equinox. Sacred to the Sun, the Irish called it the "physician's strength," as its diuretic shoots were a prized remedy for all surfeits and diseases arising from the urinary tract and kidneys. Its yellow flowers symbolize the young Sun of the Spring Equinox. Use the plant to sweep the surrounding area when working magick outside. Use in purification incenses and hang a little of the herb in your magick room as a protection. Raise the winds by throwing the herb into the air, preferably off a mountaintop, and calm the winds by burning the herb.

Bryony (*Bryonia alba, B. dioica*)

Folk Names: English mandrake, wood vine, briony, tetterberry, white bryony, tamus, ladies' sea, wild hops, wild vine

Gender: Hot

Planet: Mars

Element: Earth

Associated Deities: Isis, Kuan Yin, Jupiter, Ra, Osiris, Horus, Hermes

Part Used: Roots. POISONOUS

Specific Uses: I do not recommend using this herb at all. Traditionally, the roots were often used in place of the rather rare mandrake root. A bryony root was set on a piece of money during the full moon to cause one's riches to grow.

Buchu (*Agathosma betulina*)

Folk Names: Bookoo, bucco, bucku

Gender: Hot

Planet: Mars

Element: Fire

Associated Deities: Tiw, Horus, Ares, Mars

Part Used: Leaves

Basic Power: Energy

Specific Use: Leaves are used in ritual incense because of their aroma.

Burdock (*Arctium lappa*)

Folk Names: Beggar's buttons, clotburr, bardana, happy major, Hardock, burrseed, personata, great burdock, hurrburr, cocklebur

Gender: Hot

Planet: Mars

Element: Fire

Associated Deities: Ares, Horus, Tiw

Parts Used: The herb; the root dug in July the first year

Basic Powers: Protection, purification

Specific Uses: Sprinkle in the corners of your magick room to ward off negativity. Add to protection sachets of all kinds. Used as a purifying agent in incense and herbal waters. Can be steeped in the mop water used for cleaning.

Button Snake Root (*Liatris specata*)

Folk Names: Backache root, gay feather, blazing star,
colic root, Devil's bit

Gender: Cold

Planet: Venus

Element: Earth/Air

Associated Deities: Aphrodite, Venus, Hathor, Kuan
Yin, Freyja, Brigid, Cordelia

Part Used: Root

Basic Powers: Love, creativity, friendship

Cactus (*Cactaceae* var.)

Gender: Hot

Planet: Mars

Element: Fire

Associated Deities: Thor, Odin, Zeus, Isis, Morrigan,
Horus, Osiris

Parts Used: The entire living plant; spines

Basic Power: Protection

Specific Uses: Grow in the garden and inside the
house as a safeguard against burglary and unwanted
intrusions. The spines are used like pins in image
magick, to mark or write symbols on images of wax
or roots. Such uses are usually restricted to the more
negative aspects of image magick. However, they can
be used to mark spots of ill health, in eradication of

tumors or diseases. Fill a small jar with cacti spines, rusty nails, old tacks, and pine needles. Add rue and rosemary leaves to fill the jar; seal tightly and then bury under your doorstep as a powerful protective device.

Calamus (*Acorus calamus*)

Folk Names: Sweet flag, sweet sedge, sweet rush, aromatic rush

Gender: Cold

Planet: Moon

Element: Water

Associated Deities: Hecate, Diana, Isis

Parts Used: The herb, especially the root

Basic Powers: Protection, knowledge, binding

Specific Uses: The root is gathered in late autumn or early spring, and used for its aroma and fixative properties in perfumery and potpourris. When used as a strewing herb, it subtly perfumes the room. Can be substituted for cinnamon, nutmeg, and ginger.

Calendula (*Calendula officinalis*)

Folk Names: Pot marigold, Mary gowles, marigold

Gender: Hot

Planet: Sun

Element: Fire

Associated Deities: Selene, Luna, Ra

Part Used: Flowers

Basic Powers: Love, clairvoyance, healing

Specific Uses: The blossoms are a golden orange color. Often used in healing salves.

Camphor (*Cinnamomum camphora*)

Gender: Cold

Planet: Moon

Element: Water

Associated Deities: Isis, Khonsu, Hecate, Morrigan

Part Used: The gum. POISONOUS.

Basic Powers: None

Specific Uses: Use its odor in spells to turn away unwanted lovers. Use a drop or two in incenses to produce sleep. However, it is toxic in large quantities.

Capsicum: *See Pepper.*

Caraway (*Carum carvi*)

Folk Names: Carcum, carvi

Gender: Hot

Planet: Mercury

Element: Air

Associated Deities: Hermes, Thoth, Maat, Anubis, Odin

Parts Used: Seeds

Basic Powers: Protection, passion

Specific Uses: Use in sachet bags for protection. Add to love sachets and charms to attract a love in the physical aspect of that word. Carry the seeds in a little pouch to strengthen the memory. It was at one time used in spells to cure fickleness in lovers.

Cardamom (*Elettaria cardamomum*)

Folk Names: Ebil, capalaga, ilachi, ailu, grains of paradise

Gender: Hot

Planet: Mercury

Element: Earth/Air

Associated Deities: Mercury, Hermes, Thoth, Anubis, Maat, Odin, Oghma

Parts Used: Dried ripe seeds

Basic Powers: Love, creativity, divination, prediction

Specific Uses: It has a powerful, aromatic odor when crushed for incense or sachets.

Carnation (*Dianthus caryophyllus*)

Folk Names: Gilliflower, Jove's flower

Gender: Hot

Planet: Sun

Element: Fire

Associated Deities: Osiris, Horus, Apollo, Bast, Sekhmet

Parts Used: Flowers

Basic Powers: Protection, energy

Specific Uses: It was once worn by witches to prevent untimely death on the scaffold. It is used in power incenses and placed on the altar to produce added energy. Dry nine red carnations in the Sun, crumble them, and separate from the stems. Pour one dram of carnation oil over them; mix well and burn slowly on charcoal for a tremendously powerful incense that produces tons of energy.

Cascara Sagrada (*Rhamnus purshianus*)

Folk Names: Sacred bark

Gender: Hot

Planet: Sun

Element: Fire

Associated Deities: Ra, Horus, Apollo, Adonis

Parts Used: Bark

Basic Powers: Health, purification, power

Specific Uses: The bark is collected in the spring and early summer; it has to be stored for at least one year before it can be used. It is then used in incenses of power and purification.

Cascarilla (*Croton eleuteria*)

Folk Names: Sweetwood bark, sweet bark, Elutherica, aromatic quinquina, false quinquina

Gender: Cold

Planet: Moon

Element: Water

Associated Deities: Isis, Khonsu, Neith, Diana, Hecate, Selene, Luna, Morrighan

Part Used: Dried bark

Basic Powers: Psychic vision, divinations, magick

Specific Uses: When burned as incense, the odor resembles weak musk, being agreeable and aromatic. If the smoke is inhaled, it can cause mild intoxication but the practice is not recommended.

Cassia (*Cinnamomum cassia*)

Gender: Hot

Planet: Sun, sometimes Mercury

Element: Fire

Associated Deities: Ra, Horus, Apollo, Adonis

Part Used: Bark

Basic Powers: Protection, healing, success

Specific Uses: The dried bark can be used as a substitute for cinnamon in perfumery, potpourris, and incense. It was often burned in temples and private homes for protection and healing.

Catnip (*Nepeta cataria*)

Folk Names: Field Balm, Catmint, Catnap, Cat's Wort, Nip, Catsup

Gender: Cold

Planet: Venus

Element: Water

Associated Deity: Bast

Part Used: Herb

Basic Powers: Love, animal contacts (both physical and astral)

Specific Uses: Once chewed by warriors for fierceness in battle. Dry large leaves to use as bookmarks for magickal books. Give to your cat to create a psychic link between you two. Use in love sachets and incenses, especially with rose petals.

Cayenne (*Capsicum annum*)

Gender: Hot

Planet: Mars

Element: Fire

Associated Deities: Ares, Tiw

Part Used: Pepper, seeds

Basic Powers: Cleansing, purification

Specific Uses: Cayenne can be used in a very light coating into wounds and cuts to help stop bleeding. It will sting only in areas of many exposed nerve endings, not in the average cut or gash. For the iron-poor, an old recipe for a blood building tonic: ¼ teaspoon of cayenne in ½ cup grape juice; you can build up to one teaspoon cayenne. Drink one to three times a day. A few grains of cayenne along with sea salt can be used in a neti pot for sinus relief. *See also Pepper.*

Cedar *Cedrus libani,* Cedar of Lebanon, the Old World species; *Thuja accidentalis,* yellow cedar or Arbor Vitae, Tree of life; *Juniperus virginiana,* red cedar

Folk Names: Tree of life, arbor vitae, cedar of Lebanon

Gender: Hot

Planet: Jupiter

Element: Fire/Water

Associated Deities: Astarte, Jupiter

Parts Used: Wood, branches, oil

Basic Powers: Purification, exorcism

Specific Uses: This was used by ancient Egyptians, Babylonians, Greeks, and others as an offertory incense and burned during sacrifices. It was sacred to Astarte and associated with the Summer Solstice. Several Native American peoples burn it to repel evil spirits and to attract good ones. The tree represents sovereignty, power, and longevity. Sacred to Jupiter. Fresh cedar branches are used as brooms in purification and exorcisms in a temple or area. Cedarwood oil was a preservative used by the ancient Celts and others to preserve trophy heads. Red cedar needles and oil are used in perfumery and the sawdust in incense making.

Celandine (*Chelidonium majus, C. minus, Ranunculus ficaria*)

Folk Names: Tetterwort, Garden Celandine, greater Celandine, Chelidonum, Devil's milk, swallow herb, swallow-wort, Celydoyne, figwort, pilewort, smallwort

Gender: Hot

Planet: Sun

Element: Fire

Associated Deities: Bast, Ra, Horus, Apollo

Part Used: Herb

Basic Powers: Protection, escape

Specific Uses: It should be gathered when the Sun is in Leo and the Moon is in Aries, according to some old herbals. Aids in escaping unwarranted imprisonment and entrapments of every kind. Wear next to the skin and replace every three days. It imparts joy and good spirits if worn, and is said to cure depression.

Celery (*Apium graveolens*)

Folk Names: Smallage, smilage

Gender: Cold

Planet: Moon

Element: Water

Associated Deities: Isis, Khonsu, Diana, Hecate

Parts Used: Seeds, roots, leaves

Basic Powers: Protection, love

Specific Uses: History says that some ate it to prevent cramps. It is considered by others to be an aphrodisiac, and was mixed with some dangerous herbs for that purpose.

Centaury (*Centaurium erythraea*)

Folk Names: Century, bitter herb, lesser centaury, feverwort, Christ's ladder

Gender: Hot

Planet: Sun

Element: Fire

Associated Deities: Ra, Horus, Apollo, Adonis

Part Used: The flowering herb

Basic Power: Protection

Specific Use: Burned as incense for protection against wicked spirits.

Chamomile (*Anthemis nobilis, Matricaria chamomilla*)

Folk Names: Maythen, manzanilla, chamaimelon, camamyle, ground apple, whig plant, Roman chamomile, wild chamomile, dog chamomile

Gender: Hot

Planet: Sun

Element: Water

Associated Deities: Bast, Ra, Horus, Apollo

Parts Used: The flowers. Dog chamomile is a common wild species that has a horrible odor. Roman chamomile smells like freshly cut apples.

Basic Powers: Prosperity, meditation, sleep

Specific Uses: Use in prosperity charms to attract money. Add to incenses intended to bring on restful states for meditation and sleep. It can induce sleep if taken as a tea. It was revered by the ancient Egyptians, who used it for many purposes, including in massage oil. It was a common medieval strewing herb for its wonderful aroma. It can also be added to magickal floor washes.

Charcoal

Specific Uses: The appropriate charcoal is easily found in New Age shops; pieces are meant to be burned in a vessel filled with sand, as sand makes it easy to remove old ashes. An old recipe for making your own charcoal uses the ashes of willow, or the very fine sawdust of cedar, fir, or other trees. Crush and make into blocks by using a binding agent of egg white, gum arabic, or tragacanth. Mix into a fairly stiff paste; spread into a shallow tray and score into squares of about one-half inch for breaking. Leave to dry thoroughly.

Cherry, Wild (*Prunus avium, P. serotina, P. virginiana*)

Folk Names: Black cherry, chokecherry

Gender: Cold

Planet: Venus

Element: Earth/Air

Associated Deities: Apollo, Freyja, Ra

Parts Used: Wood, bark, fruit

Basic Powers: Creativity, health

Specific Use: One of the nine woods included in the Sabbath fires

Chestnut (*Castanea vesca, Fagua castanes*)

Folk Names: Sweet chestnut, Jupiter's nut, Husked nut

Gender: Hot

Planet: Jupiter

Element: Fire/Water

Associated Deities: Jupiter, Apollo, Odin

Parts Used: Leaves, fruit, wood

Basic Power: Healing

Specific Uses: Sacred to Jupiter, the leaves and wood were burned as incense. The fruit was used medicinally.

Cicely, Sweet (*Myrrhis odorata*)

Folk Names: British myrrh

Gender: Hot

Planet: Sun

Element: Water

Associated Deities: Isis, Ra, Adonis

Parts Used: The herb, seeds, root

Basic Power: Love

Specific Uses: It smells like the herb myrrh. The essence is said to be an aphrodisiac.

Cinnamon (*Cinnamomum verum, C. zeylanicum, C. cassia*)

Folk Names: Sweet wood, cassia

Gender: Hot

Planet: Sun

Element: Fire

Associated Deities: Ra, Horus, Apollo

Parts Used: Bark, oil

Basic Powers: Protection, healing, passion

Specific Uses: Burn to raise very high spiritual vibrations. Use in healing incenses; burn to stimulate clairvoyance. Add to prosperity mixtures. Mix with myrrh for a good general working incense. The bark is used extensively in perfumery, sachets, and incense. It was used in the embalming process in Egypt. In Arabia, its oil was used to anoint sacred ritual vessels. Medieval Europeans used it as an aphrodisiac, and the distilled water was a love potion. The aroma is sexually stimulating.

Cinquefoil (*Potentilla canadensis* or *P. reptana*)

Folk Names: Five-finger grass, five-finger blossom, sunfield, synkefoyle, five-fingers

Gender: Hot

Planet: Jupiter

Element: Earth

Part Used: Herb

Associated Deities: Zeus, the Dagda, Thor, Amun

Basic Powers: Protection, love, prosperity, healing

Specific Uses: Frogs were said to enjoy sitting around this herb. It was an ingredient in many medieval spells and love divinations. Hang at the door as a protection. Use in all incense for prosperity, purification, and protection. Cinquefoil represents love, money, health, power, and wisdom, thus making it an all-purpose magickal herb. To make a good prosperity sachet, mix together equal parts cinquefoil, cinnamon, cloves, lemon balm, and add a whole vanilla or tonka bean. Put this mixture into a rich purple cloth bag and carry to increase riches.

Citronella (*Cymbopogon nardus*)

Folk Names: Citronella grass, lemongrass

Gender: Hot

Element: Sun

Element: Fire

Associated Deities: Ra, Osiris, Horus, Apollo

Parts Used: Leaves

Basic Powers: Love, attraction

Specific Uses: It is used in perfumery, cosmetics, and soaps.

Clary Sage (*Salvia sclarea*)

Gender: Cold

Element: Water

Associated Deities: Isis, Diana, Neith, Morrigan

Parts Used: Seeds, oil

Basic Powers: Love, magick

Specific Use: The oil is a fixative in perfumes; it resembles ambergris.

Cloves (*Eugenia caryophyllata*, *Caryophyllus aromaticus*, *Syzygium aromaticum*).

Gender: Hot

Planet: Sun

Element: Fire

Associated Deities: Ra, Horus, Apollo, Osiris

Part Used: Undeveloped flower buds

Basic Powers: Protection, memory

Specific Uses: The undeveloped flowers are used in incense, potpourris, pomanders, and perfumes. It is worn to drive away hostile and negative forces and to stop gossip. Carry to strengthen the memory, and add to sachets for attracting the opposite sex. Apply a drop of clove oil to a sore tooth to stop the pain.

Clove pink (*Dianthus caryophyllus*)

Folk Names: Carnation, gilly flower

Planets: Jupiter, the Moon

Specific Uses: The tincture is used for headaches and other nervous disorders, according to Culpeper. Also used to cleanse the blood and as a remedy for gout and all aches and pains of the joints. It also promotes perspiration during fevers.

Clover (*Trifolium* spp.)

Folk Names: Trefoil, purple clover, honeystalks, three-leaved grass

Gender: Hot

Planet: Mercury

Elements: All four elements

Associated Deities: Thoth, Hermes, Maat

Parts Used: Herb and blossoms. Clover blossoms can be yellow, white, or reddish in color; usage is determined by color.

Basic Power: Healing

Specific Uses: Called *meli (honey)* and *lotos (clover)* by the Greeks. The three-leaved clover is often used in rituals designed to protect or to one looking youthful and fair. Carry one for protection. Four-leaved clovers are also carried to avoid military service. Remember to leave something in payment to the earth if you take an entire plant.

Club Moss (*Lycopodium clavatum*)

Folk Names: Foxtails, wolf claw, staghorn

Gender: Cold

Planet: Mercury

Element: Air

Associated Deities: Hermes, Thoth, Anubis, Maat

Parts Used: The herb, spores

Basic Power: Protection

Specific Uses: This is one of the sacred herbs of the Druids, and could be collected by a true priest or priestess dressed in white after a purification bath in a running stream; offerings of bread and wine were made, and the herb was cut by a silver dagger. It is an herb of great blessings and protection. The spores were collected in July and August, and the fresh plants were used in spells.

Coltsfoot (*Tussilago farfara*)

Folk Names: Coughwort, foal's foot, horsehoof, foolwort, donnhav

Gender: Cold

Planet: Venus

Element: Earth/Air

Associated Deities: Hathor, Brigid, Freyja

Parts Used: Flowers, leaves

Basic Power: Health

Specific Uses: Flowers were gathered in February, the leaves in June and early July. It was used in a mixture called British Herb Tobacco for relief of asthma and bronchitis; the mixture was predominantly coltsfoot plus buckbean, eyebright, betony, rosemary, thyme, lavender, and chamomile. A tea made from the leaves was also made for stubborn coughs.

Comfrey (*Symphytum officinale*)

Folk Names: Yalluc, slippery root, boneset, assear, consolida, healing herb, gum plant, consound bruisewort, knitbone, wallwort, black herb, healing blade

Gender: Cold

Planet: Saturn

Element: Air

Associated Deities: Nephthy, Isis, Demeter, Hecate

Parts Used: Herb, root

Basic Powers: Health, protection

Specific Uses: Carry some to ensure safety while traveling. Also put in your luggage to ensure its safety.

Copal Gum (*Protium copal*)

Folk Names: Copalquahuitl, copali

Gender: Hot

Planet: Jupiter

Element: Fire/Water

Associated Deities: Jupiter, Zeus, Ra, Osiris

Part Used: Resin

Basic Powers: Prosperity

Specific Uses: Of Mexican origin, this is a fragrant, translucent white resin distilled for Copalquahuitl, the Mexican copali incense. Originally found in Mexico, it has now been found in Zanzibar, West Africa, Mozambique, Madagascar, and India.

Coriander (*Coriandrum sativum*)

Folk Names: Cilantro, culantoo, Chinese parsley

Gender: Hot

Planet: Mars

Element: Fire

Associated Deities: Tiw, Horus

Part Used: Seeds

Basic Power: Love

Specific Uses: This plant has long been used in love
    sachets and charms. The seeds become very fragrant
    when dried and are used in perfumery and incense;
    the longer they are kept, the more aromatic they
    become. It was believed in China that these seeds
    offer immortality.

Corn (*Zea mays*)

Folk Names: Maize, maze

Gender: Hot

Planet: Sun

Element: Fire

Associated Deities: Horus, Ra, Adonis, Sekhmet, Isis

Part Used: Seed

Basic Power: Healing

Specific Uses: Corn is easily digested by the body.
    Cornbread has more nourishment than wheat bread;
    this makes it suitable for those with liver or kidney
    disorders.

Costmary (*Tanacetum balsamita*)

Folk Names: Alecost, balsam herb, Herbe Sainte Maria

Gender: Hot

Planet: Jupiter

Element: Fire/Water

Associated Deities: Jupiter, Ra, Zeus, Osiris

Part Used: Leaves

Basic Powers: Prosperity, success

Specific Uses: The leaves have a soft balsamic odor and are used in sachets.

Cowslip (*Primula veris*)

Folk Names: Marsh marigold, water dragon, palsywort

Gender: Cold

Planet: Venus

Element: Earth/Air

Associated Deities: Astarte, Freyja, Hathor, Brigid

Part Used: Flowers

Basic Powers: Visions, love

Specific Uses: Cowslip wine is slightly narcotic, so perhaps the wine enables the user to have visions. It was said that this herb would allow one entry into Freyja's pleasure palace. The pendant flowers do resemble a bunch of keys.

Cubeb (*Piper cubeba*)

Folk Names: Java pepper, tailed pepper

Gender: Hot

Planet: Mars

Element: Fire

Associated Deities: Horus, Ares, Tiw

Part Used: Unripe fruit

Basic Powers: Protection, physical attraction

Specific Uses: The dried unripe fruits are burned in incense to drive away evil spirits (don't do this in an enclosed space!) and are carried with one to melt the heart of even the coldest person. It is said to make all you meet look upon you with desire.

Cucumber (*Cucumis sativus*)

Gender: Cold

Planet: Moon

Element: Water

Associated Deities: Isis Khensu, Neith, Hecate, Morrigan

Parts Used: Fruit, seeds

Basic Powers: Healing, fertility

Specific Uses: Add the seeds to a lunar incense. It is said to help with fertility if the seeds are kept in the bedroom; replace every seven days.

Cyclamen (*Cyclamen europaeum, Cylclamen* spp.)

    Folk Names: Sow bread, groundbread, swinebread, love plant

    Gender: Cold

    Planet: Venus

    Element: Water

    Associated Deities: Hecate, Venus

    Part Used: Herb

    Basic Powers: Love, fertility, protection

    Specific Uses: Grow in the bedroom as protection while sleeping. Carry the blossoms to remove the grief of an ended love affair. Grow outside to protect the garden and the house. The flowers can also be carried to aid in fertility matters.

Cypress (*Cupressus sempervirens*)

    Folk Names: Tree of Death

    Gender: Cold

    Planet: Saturn

    Element: Earth

    Associated Deities: Mithras, Aphrodite, Ashtoreth, Pluto, Persephone, Hercules, Saturn, Artemis

    Parts Used: Branches, wood

    Basic Powers: Protection, consecration

Specific Uses: It symbolizes death, resurrection,
forgetfulness and was often used in funerals.
There was a sacred cypress cult that celebrated the
mysteries of Hercules and his mother Aphrodite in
ancient Minoan culture. Make a fire of cypress and
consecrate ritual objects in its smoke. Hang up a
small bough for protection. Add to incenses used
during the waning moon or during Winter Solstice.
Carry leaves with you to become illuminated
concerning death in all its aspects.

Damiana (*Turnera aphrodisiaca*)

Folk Names: Turnera diffusa

Gender: Cold

Planet: Venus

Element: Earth/Air

Associated Deities: Venus, Aphrodite, Hathor, Freyja

Part Used: Leaves

Basic Powers: Fertility, love

Specific Uses: Smells a little like minty chamomile.
The leaves are said to be a powerful aphrodisiac.
However, I do NOT recommend ingesting this herb
in any form.

Dammar Gum (Var., from *Vateria indica, Canarium strictum*)

Folk Names: Damar, black dhup, black dammar

Planet: Mercury

Element: Earth/Air

Associated Deities: Hermes, Thoth, Maat

Parts Used: Resin, gum

Basic Powers: Divination, prediction

Specific Uses: A Malayan resin from the genus *Dammara*. Damars were once used for caulking ships. White Dammar is from the genus *Vateria indica*, while the Black Dammar is from the genus *Canarium strictum*. Usually in powder form, this resin is used in making incense cones.

Dandelion (*Taraxacum officinale*)

Folk Names: Cankerwort, wild endive, lion's tooth, blow ball, piss weed

Gender: Hot

Planet: Jupiter

Element: Fire/Water

Associated Deities: Jupiter, Zeus, Amun, the Dagda

Parts Used: Leaves, root

Basic Powers: Divination, healing

Specific Uses: A sign of approaching rain is when the down blows off the dandelion when there is no wind. People blow the seeds off to carry their thoughts to their loved ones. Used in a bath, it is said to strengthen the psychic talents and the ability to summon spirits. The roots and leaves have a harsh bitter smell and taste but are said to help with uterine infections.

Datura (*Datura stramonium*)

Folk Names: Thorn apple, stramonium, jimson weed, devil's apple, nightshade, mad-apple, stinkwort

Gender: Hot

Planet: Sun

Element: Fire

Associated Deities: Horus, Ra, Apollo, Lugh, Bel

Parts Used: Leaves and seed. POISONOUS.

Basic Powers: Scrying, visions, prophecy

Specific Uses: This is a poisonous and narcotic herb used by shamans. Inhaling the fumes is a shamanic aid to incantations and an ingredient in scrying incense. It is said that the Romani smoked the leaves for visions, and the priests of Apollo at Delphi used it in a drink for prophecies. Traditions say that gamblers once nibbled on the seeds to become

clairvoyant and dream about the ending for a night
of gaming. This herb contains the same alkaloids
as nightshade. Early Arabian names were *datora*
and *tatorsh*. Early Sanskrit writings refer to this
drug as *dhurstura* and *unmata*. Old Chinese herbal
medical texts state that if equal amounts of datura
and *Cannibis sativa* were gathered in the seventh and
eighth moons of the lunar year, dried in the shade,
then pulverized in wine, drinking the resulting
preparation would allow surgery and cauterization
with little or no pain.

Deer's Tongue (*Frasera speciosa*, *Liatris odoratissima*)

Folk Name: Wild vanilla

Gender: Cold

Planet: Venus

Element: Earth/Air

Associated Deities: Aphrodite, Hathor, Freyja

Part Used: Leaves

Basic Power: Love

Specific Uses: The leaves are used in potpourris for
their fragrance, and in small amounts to flavor
tobacco. Sprinkle the bottom of your shoes with
deer's tongue, and no one can speak against you.

Devil's Bit: *See Unicorn Root, True.*

Dill: (*Anethum graveolens, Peucedanum graveolens*)

Folk Names: Dill weed, Aneton, dilly, garden dill

Gender: Hot

Planet: Mercury

Element: Fire

Associated Deities: Zeus, Osiris, Isis, Odin, Kuan Ti, Agni, Indra

Parts Used: Herb, seeds

Basic Powers: Protection, love

Specific Uses: The dried ripe fruits were used by medieval magicians in spells and charms against witchcraft. It can be used in love sachets. Tie up the dried seed heads as protection of your home and property. Also use the seeds in protection sachets and incenses. Some mistake this herb for the herb anise, whose top also has an umbrella shape; anise, however, has a distinctively different odor.

Use the seed to make a cordial to relieve digestive problems, flatulence, headaches, and insomnia. In medieval times the seeds were chewed to freshen the breath and allay hunger pains. Dill water was given to babies for colic.

Dittany of Crete: (*Origanum dictamnus*)

Folk Names: Hop marjoram

Gender: Cold

Planet: Mercury

Element: Earth/Air

Associated Deities: Hermes, Thoth, Anubis, Maat

Part Used: Herb

Basic Powers: Divination, manifestation

Specific Uses: It is a powerful magickal fumigation herb, and an excellent base for evocation manifestations when burned as incense.

Dogwood (*Cornus florida*)

Folk Names: Cornel, boxwood, dogtree, green ozier

Gender: Cold

Planet: Moon

Element: Water

Associated Deities: Bran the Blessed, Saturn

Parts Used: Wood, bark, fruit

Specific Uses: The tree yields a red dye. When it flowered, it was a sign to plant corn.

Dragon's Blood (*Daemonorops draco, Dracaena draco*)

Folk Names: Calamus draco

Gender: Hot

Planet: Mars

Element: Fire

Associated Deities: Agni, Horus, Hecate, Isis, Maat

Parts Used: Gum, also the fruit's resinous secretions

Basic Powers: Energy, purification, protection

Specific Uses: Add a pinch of the ground herb in incenses to increase their potency and effectiveness. Add to love incenses and sachets. A piece of the resin placed under the mattress was used to cure impotency. Dragon's Blood ink is a good tool to use when drawing talismans and sigils; simply dissolve a small amount of powder in a little alcohol.

Echincea (*Echinacea angustifolia, E. purpurea*)

Folk Names: Cone flower, rudbeckia, Black Sampson

Gender: Cold

Planet: Moon

Element: Earth/Water

Associated Deities: Demeter, Gaea, Apollo

Parts Used: Dried root; rhizome

Basic Powers: Healing

Specific Uses: The flower may be harvested after the seeds mature on the cone, but the petals are still present. The root also can be used. This herb increases the body's resistance to infection. Its action is antiseptic and can be taken in capsule form for boils, cancer, and other blood impurities.

Elder (*Sambucus canadensis*)

Folk Names: Devil's eye, lady elder, Frau Holla, hollunder, ellhorn, pipe tree, boure tree, sweet elder, tree of doom, black elder, elderberry

Gender: Cold

Planet: Venus

Element: Air

Associated Deities: Holda, Venus, Bertha, Hecate

Parts Used: Leaves, berries, flowers

Basic Powers: Purification, love

Specific Uses: Has a mixed reputation, depending on the locality. Sometimes a symbol of death and grief. The Druids used it to both bless and curse by scattering the leaves to the winds in the four directions. Sacred to the Great Goddess, Venus, and the Summer Solstice. Tradition says that standing under an elder at this time enables one to see fairies. Its odor is said to be narcotic and vision-inducing.

Elder wands are used for evoking and exorcising evil spirits. The branches can be made into panpipes and flutes. Said to ward off bad luck, thieves, and lightning.

Elder, dwarf (*Sambucus ebulus*)

Folk Names: Water elder, whitten, Guelder Rose, danewort, walewort, blood hilder

Gender: Cold

Planet: Venus

Element: Air

Associated Deities: Holda, Venus, Bertha, Hecate

Parts Used: Leaves, berries, flowers

Basic Powers: Purification, love

Specific Uses: Same as elder.

Elecampane (*Inula helenium*)

Folk Names: Scabwort, nurse-heal, elfwort, abycompaine, elfdock, horse-heal

Gender: Hot

Planet: Mercury

Element: Water

Associated Deities: Hathor, Freyja, Branwen, Adonis, Tammuz

Parts Used: Roots, leaves

Specific Uses: In ancient times it was regarded as a general cure-all as well as being used in love potions, sachets, and incense, usually mixed with vervain and mistletoe.

Elemi Gum (*Canarium luzonicum*)

Gender: Cold

Planet: Venus

Element: Earth/Air

Associated Deities: Hathor, Freyja, Astarte

Parts Used: Resin, gum

Basic Powers: Creativity, love

Specific Uses: Elemi oil is known as Elemin; it is obtained from the tree *Canarium commune* from Manila, the *Icica icicaribe* from Brazil, and the *Elaphium elemiferum* from Mexico. Used in incense.

Elm (*Ulmus campestris*)

Folk Names: English elm, slippery elm, Indian elm, rock elm, sweet elm, winged elm

Gender: Cold

Planet: Saturn

Element: Earth

Associated Deities: Dionysus, Isis, Demeter, Hecate, Saturn, Cerridwen

Parts Used: Leaves, bark

Basic Powers: Knowledge, protection

Specific Use: In Ireland this tree is a substitute for the silver fir as ruler of the Winter Solstice.

Ergot (*Claviceps purpurea*)

Folk Names: Mother of rye, hornseed, smut rye

Gender: Cold

Planet: Mercury

Associated Deities: Hermes, Thoth, Anubis, Maat, Odin

Parts Used: Fungus. POISONOUS.

Specific Uses: This fungus is a disease that attacks grasses, especially rye and wheat. It contains LSD and was used for its hallucinogenic properties in the Eleusinian Mysteries. I do NOT recommend its use.

Eucalyptus (*Eucalyptus globulus*)

Folk Names: Blue gum

Gender: Cold

Planet: Moon

Element: Air

Associated Deities: Apollo, Thoth, Brigid

Parts Used: Leaves, pods, oil

Basic Power: Healing

Specific Uses: The oil of the leaves is a powerful antiseptic that can be used to sterilize instruments. It also helps fight off colds and flu germs if burned in an aromatherapy vessel. Stuff healing poppets and small pillows with the leaves. Ring blue candles with the leaves and burn for healing vibrations.

Euphorbia (*Euphorbia resinifera*)

Folk Names: Spurge, gum thistle

Gender: Hot

Planet: Mars, sometimes Mercury

Element: Air

Associated Deities: Hermes, Thoth, Maat, Anubis, Thor

Part Used: Resinous juice

Basic Powers: Protection, divination, conjuration

Specific Uses: Used in ointments and potions. Under the rule of Mars, it can be used for death and destruction magick.

Eyebright (*Euphrasia officinalis*)

Folk Names: Euphrosyne, red eyebright

Gender: Hot

Planet: Sun, occasionally Venus or Mercury

Element: Air

Associated Deities: Isis, Great Goddess, Thoth, Merlin

Parts Used: Herb

Basic Powers: Clairvoyance, healing

Specific Uses: Brew a mild potion with water to wash out the eyes when irritated. Anoint the eyelids daily for clairvoyant visions.

Fennel (*Foeniculum vulgare*)

Folk Name: Sweet fennel

Gender: Cold

Planets: Mercury, occasionally the Moon

Element: Earth/Air

Associated Deities: Thoth, Hermes, Anubis, Maat

Parts Used: Herb, seeds

Basic Power: Protection

Specific Uses: The plant is a preventative against evil influences and was hung over doors along with St. John's wort on Summer Solstice eve to ward off evil spirits. It is also said to confer longevity, strength, and courage.

Fern (*Pteris aquilina*)

Folk Names: Bracken, female fern, brake fern, brakeroot, common polypody, stone brake

Gender: Cold

Planet: Saturn

Element: Earth

Associated Deities: Saturn, Hecate, Odin, Osiris

Parts Used: Fronds, root

Basic Powers: Protection, love

Specific Uses: The Druids classed this plant as one of their sacred trees. Setting growing bracken on fire is an old custom for producing rain. Its smoke drives away serpents, gnats, and other noxious night creatures of the swamps; it is also used in incenses of exorcism.

Fern (All species)

Gender: Hot and cold, depending upon the intent

Planet: Saturn

Element: Earth

Part Used: Herb

Basic Powers: Protection, love

Specific Uses: All ferns give extremely powerful protection. Throw fern fronds on hot coals to send out an aura of protection. Also burn outdoors to bring rain. The unexpanded fronds of the male fern are dried over a Summer Solstice fire and kept for protection. These "lucky hands" are rare today.

Feverfew (*Chrysanthemum parthenium* or *Pyrethrum parthenium*)

Folk Names: pyrethrum, featherfoil, Flirtwort

Gender: Cold

Planet: Venus

Element: Earth/Air

Associated Deities: Aphrodite, Astarte, Hathor, Freyja

Part Used: Herb

Basic Powers: Protection, purification

Specific Uses: It is planted around houses to purify the atmosphere and ward off disease. When worn, it is thought to prevent sickness and accidents.

Fig (*Ficus carica*)

Folk Names: Common fig

Gender: Hot

Planet: Jupiter

Element: Fire

Associated Deities: Great Goddess, Bacchus, Saturn, Zeus

Parts Used: Fruit, milky sap of the stalk

Basic Powers: Love, strength

Specific Uses: In Crete, this tree was sacred to the Goddess; wreaths of fig leaves were worn during

Saturn rituals and were traditional New Year's gifts. Greek athletes ate figs to increase strength and swiftness; they are also said to be an aphrodisiac.

Fir, Silver (*Abies alba*)

Folk Names: Birth tree

Gender: Hot

Planet: Jupiter

Element: Fire

Associated Deities: Artemis, Selene, Athena, Druantis

Parts Used: Branches, needles, sap

Basic Powers: Protection, knowledge

Specific Uses: The birth tree of Northern Europe, where a flaming fir candle was whirled three times around a birthing bed soon after delivery; this custom was believed to bless and protect mother and child. In Greece this tree was sacred to the Moon Goddess. It ruled the first day of the Celtic year, December 24. There was a Gallic Fir Goddess, Druantia, called "Queen of the Druids," who was the mother of the tree calendar.

Flax (*Linum usitatissimum*)

Folk Name: Linseed

Gender: Cold

Planet: Mercury

Element: Earth/Air

Associated Deity: Hulda

Parts Used: Herb, seeds

Basic Power: Protection

Specific Uses: Linen was made from this plant in
Egypt. The plant is under the protection of Hulda,
the Teutonic goddess who taught mortals the arts
of spinning and weaving. It is a protection against
sorcery. It is kept in the home to protect it from
disturbing outside influences and promotes peace.

Fly Agaric (*Amanita muscaria*)

Folk Name: Death Angel

Gender: Cold

Planet: Saturn

Element: Earth

Associated Deities: Nephthys, Isis, Hecate, Cerridwen,
Saturn

Parts Used: Fungus. POISONOUS.

Basic Power: Clairvoyance

Specific Uses: This magick mushroom has been used in
secret rituals all over the world. It was brewed into a tea
and drunk directly before admission to certain rituals.

Foxglove (*Digitalis purpurea*)

Folk Names: Digitalis, Fairy Gloves, Dead Men's Bells, Fairy Fingers, dog's finger, lion's mouth

Gender: Cold

Planet: Venus

Element: Earth/Air

Associated Deities: Astarte, Hathor, Freyja

Parts Used: Leaves. POISONOUS.

Basic Powers: Health, creativity, imagination

Specific Uses: It is associated with fairies, and the markings on its blossoms are said to be where elves have placed their fingers.

Frangipani (*Plumeria acuminate* and *P. rubra*)

Gender: Cold

Planet: Moon

Element: Water

Associated Deities: Isis, Khonsu, Morrigan, Diana

Part Used: Flowers

Basic Power: Love

Specific Uses: Used in perfumery; burned as a love incense.

Frankincense (*Boswellia carterii* or *B. thurifera*)

Folk Names: Olibanum, Olibans, incense

Gender: Hot

Planet: Sun

Element: Fire

Associated Deities: Ra, Baal

Part Used: Gum

Basic Powers: Protection, purification, consecration, exorcism

Specific Uses: Burn to raise positive vibrations, to purify, consecrate ritual tools, protect, and exorcise. Often used in charm bags and sachets. It induces visions and aids in meditations. Burn during sunrise rituals of all kinds. Mix with cumin and burn as a powerful protective incense useful for general working. The gum resin has been used for thousands of years as an incense of high religious and ritual meaning. Egyptian Incense: frankincense, benzoin, and aloe wood. Church Incense: 10 ounces frankincense, 4 ounces powdered benzoin, and 1 ounce storax.

Fumitory (*Fumaria officinalis*)

Folk Names: Earth Smoke, beggary, nidor

Gender: Cold

Planet: Saturn

Element: Earth

Associated Deities: Kronos, Nephthys, Demeter, Hecate

Part Used: Herb

Basic Power: Exorcism

Specific Uses: Legend says that fumitory was originally created from vapors rising out of the earth. When burned, its smoke has the power of expelling evil spirits in exorcisms.

Furze (*Ulex europaeus*)

Folk Names: Gorse, broom, Frey, whim

Gender: Hot

Planet: Mars

Element: Fire

Associated Deities: Jupiter, Areas, Thor, Horus

Parts Used: Flowers, seeds

Basic Powers: Protection, battle

Specific Uses: This shrub rules the Spring Equinox, when it blooms and attracts the first bees of the year. Its golden flowers symbolize the young Sun in spring. It is sacred to Jupiter, god of shepherds.

Galangal (*Alpinia officinarum* or *Kaempferia galangal*)

Folk Names: Catarrh root, Indian root, colic root, chewing John, maraba, China root, low John

Gender: Hot

Planet: Mars, sometimes Jupiter

Element: Fire/Water

Associated Deities: Horus, Thor, Ares

Part Used: Root

Basic Powers: Energy, knowledge, psychic enhancement, good luck

Specific Uses: The root is aromatic and used in potpourris, incenses, and perfumes. Carried as a good luck charm. Its odor and taste is similar to ginger. Used in rituals for knowledge and conversation with guardian angels.

Galbanum (*Bubon galbaniferum* or *Ferula galbaniflua*)

Gender: Hot

Planet: Sun

Element: Fire

Associated Deities: Horus, Ra, Apollo, Adonis

Parts Used: Juice or gum, perhaps from the flowers or roots

Basic Powers: Success

Specific Uses: The odor is pungent and rather strong, but also makes perfumes retain their fragrance longer.

Gardenia (*Gardenia* spp.)

Gender: Cold

Planet: Moon

Element: Water

Associated Deities: Isis, Diana, Luna, Morrigan

Part Used: Flowers

Basic Powers: Love, passion

Specific Uses: Wear the flower to attract love and new friends. Dry and crush its petals, mix with ground orris root, and lightly dust the body to attract the opposite sex. Use as a link with the Moon.

Garlic (*Allium sativum*)

Folk Names: Poor man's treacle, garleac, garlicke, clove garlic

Gender: Hot

Planet: Mars

Element: Fire

Associated Deity: Hecate

Parts Used: Bulb, flower

Basic Powers: Protection, exorcism

Specific Uses: It was venerated by ancient Egyptians and placed by the Greeks on piles of stones at crossroads as a supper for Hecate. Carry garlic on trips over water to prevent drowning. Peel cloves of the fresh bulb, and put one in each room when disease threatens. Hang up in newly built homes to prevent negative energies from growing there. Add to all protective sachets; hang up a rope of garlic in the kitchen for the same reason. It is a good antibiotic and fungicide; it reduces high blood pressure and lowers cholesterol. Helps strengthen the immune system. Use a garlic poultice on a boil to draw it to a head so it can be drained.

Geranium (*Geranium* spp., *Pelargonium* spp.)

Folk Names: Alum root, wild cranesbill

Gender: Cold

Planet: Mars

Element: Water

Associated Deities: Apollo, Brigid, Freyja, Isis, Thoth, Osiris

Parts Used: Flowers, leaves

Basic Powers: Love, healing, protection

Specific Uses: The red petals are added to potpourris for color. Leaves of scented geraniums are used in perfumery and sachets. Alum Root (wild geranium) is used similarly. Wear the flowers, or add them to love sachets. The white variety is worn to promote fertility, while the red are a good protection and aid in healing. Plant in the garden (especially pink and red) to protect the house and to keep snakes away.

Ginger (*Zingiber officinale*)

Folk Names: African ginger, black ginger

Gender: Hot

Planet: Mars, possibly the Sun

Element: Fire

Associated Deities: Tiw, Thor, Horus, Ares

Part Used: Root

Basic Power: Offertory

Specific Uses: The root is placed on the altar and around a ritual circle that involves elemental spirits as an offering. The root is harvested in Asia in the autumn. Ginger is good for upset stomach, nausea, circulation, aches and pains, and is a lymph cleanser.

Ginseng (*Panax quinquefolius*)

Folk Names: Osha, Wonder of the World, Sang

Gender: Cold

Planet: Moon

Element: Water

Associated Deities: Isis, Diana, Luna, Morrigan

Part Used: Root

Basic Powers: Divination, love, health

Specific Uses: Root is highly regarded in Chinese medicine as a cure-all and rejuvenator. Taken in a syrup form or a tea, ginseng stimulates the psychic centers.

Grains of Paradise (*Ampelopsis grana paradisi*)

Folk Names: Habzeli, Hungarian pepper, paprika, sweet pepper

Gender: Hot

Planet: Mars, sometimes Jupiter

Element: Fire

Associated Deities: Thor, Mars, Ares, Horus

Parts Used: Pods, seeds

Basic Power: Protection

Specific Uses: Burn mixed with other herbs to fumigate and exorcise a place. Do not do this with other people or pets in the house.

Graveyard Dust *See Mullein* and *Valerian.*

Hawthorn (*Crataegus oxyacantha*)

Folk Names: Huath, May bush, tree of chastity, thorn, white thorn, May tree, haw

Gender: Hot

Planet: Mars

Element: Fire

Associated Deities: Cardea, Olwen, Blodeuwedd, Hecate

Parts Used: Leaves, wood

Basic Power: Protection

Specific Uses: Sacred to the May Queen and the Goddess of Flowers. Also a symbol of chastity. All temples were cleaned out in May, and the sacred images were ritually washed and decorated. The Goddess is supposed to have carried a hawthorn wand with which She worked spells; some witches also use this wood for wands of power. Known as the fairy tree, it blooms only around the first of May. The flowers are white and fragrant, but it is unlucky to cut them and bring them into the house. This tree has been planted and used as boundary hedge in Britain since at least 1750. In autumn, the berries ripen and fall. They ferment on the ground, and birds that eat them can act drunk.

The hawthorn is tolerant of strong winds and dryness, as well as excessive moisture. The blossoms have a strong scent (said to be erotic to men), but repels bees. Symbol of white magick.

Hazel (*Corylus* spp. and *Corylus avellana*)

Folk Name: Coll

Gender: Hot

Planet: Sun

Element: Air

Associated Deities: Mercury, Thoth, Artemis, Diana

Parts Used: Nuts, wood

Basic Powers: Fertility, protection, mental powers

Specific Uses: A symbol; of concentrated wisdom, knowledge, and poetic eloquence; sacred to the Nine Muses. Druidic heralds carried hazel wands. Hazel is the most powerful tree for general magick wands, as it symbolizes white magick and healing. Forked hazel branches are used for divining buried treasure, water, thieves, and murderers. The caryatid is a type of nut fairy or nymph who gives poetic inspiration. String hazel nuts and hang up in the house for good luck. The wood serves as an anti-lightning charm. The nuts are eaten to gain wisdom. Draw a circle around yourself on the ground with a hazel twig if outside and in need of magickal protection.

Heather: (*Erica vulgaris*)

Folk Names: Heath

Gender: Cold

Planet: Venus

Element: Water

Associated Deities: Venus, Isis, Cybele

Parts Used: Flowers, oil

Basic Powers: Love, protection

Specific Uses: Rules the Summer Solstice, as it symbolizes love and passion. Sacred to Venus and red heather to Isis. Also associated with bees and their deity Cybele. White heath is a lucky charm against acts of unwanted passion.

Heather (*Calluna vulgaris*)

Folk Names: Common heather, ling, Scottish heather

Gender: Cold

Planet: Venus

Element: Water

Associated Deity: Isis

Part Used: Herb

Basic Powers: Protection, rain-making

Specific Uses: Carry as a guard against rape. Burn with fern to attract rain.

Heliotrope (*Heliotropium peruviana, H. europaeum, H. arborescens*)

Folk Names: Turnsole, cherry pie

Gender: Hot

Planet: Sun

Element: Fire

Associated Deity: Apollo

Parts Used: Flowers, leaves

Basic Powers: Clairvoyance, exorcism

Specific Uses: The flowers are wonderfully fragrant and are used in perfumery and potpourris. Put under your pillow to induce prophetic dreams, especially to discover the thief if you have been robbed. Also used in exorcism incenses and healing sachets.

Hellebore (*Helleborus niger*)

Folk Name: Christmas rose

Gender: Cold

Planet: Saturn

Element: Earth

Associated Deities: Kronos, Nephthys, Hecate

Part Used: Root. POISONOUS.

Basic Power: Visions

Specific Uses: Both the black and green varieties were used in incenses to cause frenzy. Also used in exorcism and counter-magick to protect from evil spells. I do NOT recommend using this herb.

Hemp (*Cannabis sativa, Cannabis indica*)

Folk Names: Marijuana, kif, bhand, grass, pot, weed, hashish (the resin)

Gender: Hot

Planet: Jupiter

Element: Fire/Water

Associated Deities; Zeus, Amun, the Dagda

Parts Used: The herb, resin

Basic Powers: Divination, love

Specific Uses: One old divination recipe calls for burning hemp and mugwort while gazing into crystal balls. This herb also figures in many love spells, as it is an aphrodisiac and intoxicant, with the effect varying with the individual. Its action is almost entirely on the higher nervous centers, so it alters perception and time sense.

Henbane (*Hyoscyamus niger*)

Folk Names: Hog's bean, Devil's eye, henbells, Jupiter's bean, poison tobacco

Gender: Cold

Planet: Saturn

Element: Water

Associated Deities: Hecate, Morrigan, Circe

Parts Used: Leaves, root. POISONOUS.

Basic Power: Love.

Specific Uses: It is similar to datura and nightshade
 but less powerful. Used to call up evil entities and
 increase magickal powers. Mind-altering and
 hallucinogenic.

Henna (*Lawsonia alba, L. inermis*)

Folk Names: Al-Khanna, Al-henna, Jamaica
 mignonette, Egyptian privet, Mehndi, Mendee

Gender: Cold.

Planet: Moon

Element: Water

Associated Deities: Isis, Khensu, Neither, Diana,
 Hecate, Selen, Luna, Morrighan

Parts Used: Leaves, flowers

Basic Powers: Exorcism, uncrossing

Specific Uses: Used in incense.

High John the Conqueror(*Impomoea purga, I. jalaps,
Convolvulus jalapa*)

Folk Name: Jalap

Gender: Cold

Planet: Saturn

Element: Earth

Associated Deities: Saturn, Kronos, Zeus, Isis, Maat

Part Used: Root

Basic Powers: Prosperity

Specific Uses: Anoint the root with mint oil and tie up in a green or purple bag to attract needed money. Also add the root to candle anointing oils. It is carried as a talisman against danger and trouble. It is also a charm for legal problems: consecrate a root with the four elements, sleep with it under your pillow for seven nights, then carry it into court and elsewhere with you.

Holly (*Ilex aquifolium, I. opaca*)

Folk Name: Tinne

Gender: Hot

Planet: Mars

Element: Fire

Part Used: Herb

Basic Power: Protection

Specific Uses: The boughs were used for decorating and as gifts during the Saturnalia and the Winter Solstice. Planting it near a house or farm was believed to repel poison and defend from lightning and evil.

Hollyhock (*Mallows* spp.; *Althaea rosea*, *A. officanlis*; *althaea* means "healer")

Folk Name: Garden hollyhock

Gender: Hot

Plant: Jupiter

Element: Fire/Water

Associated Deities: Jupiter, Zeus, Amun

Part Used: Flowers

Basic Power: Healing

Specific Uses: The hollyhock was brought to the United State from China and was once used as a pot herb, although it doesn't taste very good. The flowers were used as a dye when gathered in July and early August. When dried, the blossoms turn a deep purplish-black. Used medicinally for their diuretic properties. The flowers are used in infusions as a mouthwash and to treat disorders of the gums. The root is dried, ground to a power, and then boiled in wine to treat worms in children. The leaves can be used as a gargle for swollen tonsils and sore mouths.

Honey (Although technically not an herb, this nectar of flowers has always been important.)

Folk Name: Golden nectar

Specific Uses: It is best to use wildflower or herbal honey—not alfalfa or clover honey—because of the commercial pesticides used for cultivating the latter. Local honey has been shown to help cope with allergies, especially in children. Pure raw honey is an antiseptic, an emollient, a preservative, soothing, and used externally to encourage new skin growth. Increases the action of an herb with which it is mixed because of its enzymes and trace minerals. Carries herbal actions quickly into the blood, when used externally, thereby increasing the efficiency of a formula.

In the 1960s, Dr. W. G. Sacketter inoculated honey with typhoid and dysentery bacteria, hoping to prove honey was fertile ground for germs, but he only proved the opposite. Within ten hours, the dysentery bacteria were all dead, and within forty-eight house the typhoid germs were dead. Repeat trials showed the same results. Honey should never be given to infants, as their immature digestive systems allow certain strains of deadly botulism to flourish. It is safe for children over one year of age.

Honeysuckle (*Lonicera caprifolium, L. pericyenum*)

Folk Names: Woodbine

Planet: Jupiter

Element: Earth

Associated Deities: Hermes, Thoth, Isis, Freyja

Part Used: Flowers

Basic Powers: Prosperity, clairvoyance

Specific Uses: Ring green candles with the flowers to attract money. Add to all prosperity sachets. Lightly crush fresh flowers on the forehead to heighten clairvoyance powers.

Hops (*Humulus lupulus*)

Folk Names: Beer flower

Gender: Hot

Planet: Mars

Associated Deities: Apollo, Brigid

Parts Used: Fruit

Basic Powers: Healing

Specific Uses: Healing incenses and sachets. A small pillow stuffed with the dried herb helps bring on sleep.

Horehound (*Marrubium vulgare*)

Folk Names: Eye of the Star, white horehound, hoarhound, maruil, soldier's tea, seed of Horus, bull's blood, marrubium, haram, llewyd y cwn

Gender: Hot

Planet: Mercury

Element: Earth

Associated Deity: Horus

Part Used: Herb

Basic Powers: Protection, healing

Specific Uses: Put in protective sachets and incenses. Highly praised by ancient Egyptians and Romans. Brew into a strong tea for a persistent cough.

Houseleek (*Sempervivum tectorum*)

Folk Names: Hen and chickens, Aaron's rod, Jupiter's beard, thunder plant

Gender: Hot

Planet: Mars

Element: Fire

Associated Deities: Thor, Horus, Tiw, Thor

Parts Used: Leaves

Basic Powers: Energy, protection

Specific Uses: Sacred to Thor; protects the home it grows on or near from fire, storms, and lightning, while ensuring prosperity. It grows on rooftops, especially those in England and Europe. Also guards against sorcery.

Hyacinth (*Hyacinthus orientalis*)

Gender: Cold

Planet: Venus

Element: Water

Associated Powers: Love, protection

Specific Uses: Use in sachets to ease childbirth; protects and guards against nightmares. Sniff the fresh flower to relieve grief.

Hyssop (*Hyssopus officinalis*)

Folk Names: ysopo, isopo, holy herb

Gender: Hot

Planet: Jupiter

Element: Fire

Associated Deities: Zeus, Amun, Thor

Parts Used: Herb

Basic Powers: Purification, protection

Specific Uses: Add to purification bath sachets of all types; use to protect and cleanse sacred places. Druids used sprigs as water sprinklers for purification and exorcism. To ward off psychic attack, place a sprig at each window; this also keeps demons away.

Ivy (*Hedera* spp.)

Folk Name: Gort

Gender: Cold

Planet: Saturn

Element: Water

Associated Deities: Bacchus, Osiris, Dionysus, Cerridwen, Saturn

Part Used: Herb

Basic Power: Protection

Specific Uses: During the Bacchanal revels, the leaves were chewed for visions; it also symbolizes resurrection. It was used to decorate temples during Saturnalia and the Winter Solstice. It is a guardian when growing on the walls of a house or other buildings.

Jasmine (*Jasminum officinale, J. odoratissimum*)

Folk Names: Moonlight on the grove, jessamin, jessamine

Gender: Cold

Planet: Jupiter

Element: Earth

Associated Deities: Isis, Hera, Apollo

Part Used: Flowers

Basic Powers: Love, prosperity

Specific Uses: Jasmine oil comes from *J. officinale*. The
flowers of *J. odoratissimum* retain their scent when
dried. Used in love sachets and in prosperity rituals
of all kinds. Attracts spiritual love.

John the Conqueror: *See Bethroot.*

Juniper (*Juniperus communis, Juniperus* spp.)

Gender: Hot

Planet: Sun

Element: Fire

Associated Deities: Apollo, Horus, Brigid

Parts Used: Berries, branches

Basic Powers: Protection, love

Specific Uses: A holy tree in Northern Europe and
Siberia, where it is used in shamanic incense (along
with wild thyme). They use the ripe blue berries as
medicine. Known to be antibacterial, antiseptic, and
antifungal. String the mature berries for an attractive
charm, designed to draw lovers. Sometimes they
are used in anti-theft sachets. Grow juniper near
your doors for protection. Over hundreds of years

it was considered very effective against all demons.
The berries are used in seasoning of venison or
wild duck: mix with lemon, one bay leaf and 4 to 5
juniper berries. Parboil the mix in beef stock. Baste
the wild meat while it is cooking.

Karaya (*Sterculia* spp., *Cochlospermum gossypium*)

Folk Names: Katira gum

Gender: Cold

Planet: Moon

Element: Water

Associated Deities: Isis, Khensu, Kuan Yin, Neith,
Diana, Hecate, Selene, Luna, Morrighan

Part Used: Gum resin

Basic Powers: Divination, psychic vision, prophecy,
magick

Kava Kava (*Piper methysticum*)

Folk Names: Intoxicating pepper, ava pepper

Gender: Cold

Planet: Saturn

Element: Earth

Associated Deities: Saturn, Kronos, Hecate, Demeter,
Danu

Part Used: Root

Basic Power: Love

Specific Uses: The aromatic root is frequently used in love potions and sachets. Smells a little like lilac but is a hallucinogenic.

Khus Khus: *See Vetiver.*

Labdanum: *See Onycha.*

Lady's Mantle (*Alchemilla vulgaris*)

Folk Names: Lion's foot, bear's foot, nine hooks

Gender: Cold

Planet: Venus

Element: Air

Associated Deities: Hathor, Freyja, Venus

Part Used: Herb

Basic Power: Alchemy

Specific Uses: The foliage gives a subtle influence to the dew that collects in its leaves; this was gathered by alchemists for preparing the philosopher's stone.

Larch (*Larix europaea, L. decidua*)

Folk Names: European larch, common larch, Venice turpentine

Gender: Hot

Planet: Jupiter

Element: Fire/Water

Associated Deities: Jupiter, Zeus, Amun, Don, the
Dagda, Thor

Parts Used: Bark, resin, needles

Basic Powers: Honor, riches, good luck

Specific Uses: *See Pine.*

Laudanum: *See Poppy.*

Laurel (*Laurus nobilis*)

Gender: Hot

Planet: Sun

Element: Fire

Associated Deities: Apollo, Saturn, Ra, Horus

Parts Used: Leaves, bark, fruit, oil

Basic Powers: Prophecy, honor, inspiration, protection,
purification

Specific Uses: Sacred to Apollo and the Sun, laurel
garlands were given to poets, heroes, and others
who excelled in courage, service, and the creation
of beauty. The priestesses of the Triple Goddess and
the Delphic oracles chewed the leaves for prophecy.
Put them under your pillow to have visions and
poetic inspiration. They are a symbol of immortality.
Use them in love charms, perfumes, sachets, and
incenses of power, protection, purification, and
exorcism. This herb resists evils ruled by Saturn as it
counteracts negativity and restriction.

Lavender (*Lavendula officinalis, L. vera*)

   Folk Names: Spike, elf leaf

   Gender: Hot

   Planet: Mercury, sometimes Jupiter

   Element: Air

   Associated Deities: Zeus, Jupiter, Odin, Osiris, Juno, Hera, Isis

   Part Used: Flowers

   Basic Powers: Love, protection, purification

   Specific Uses: The flowers are frequently used in perfumery, sachets, potpourris, and incenses. The Egyptians and Romans used them in the baths. It is one of the ingredients in purification bath sachets. It is often an addition to healing sachets, especially bath mixtures, and is added to incenses to cause sleep. For better night relaxation, lavender-scented water can be lightly sprayed on bed sheets. It is a symbol of cleanliness and virtue. Midwives burned it in preparation for childbirth.

Lemon (*Citrus limon*)

   Folk Names: Citrus medica, citronnier, leemoo

   Gender: Cold

   Planet: Mercury

   Element: Earth/Air

Associated Deities: Hermes, Thoth, Anubis, Maat, Odin

Parts Used: Rind, juice, oil

Basic Power: Divination, prophecy, eloquence

Specific Uses: The oil, *oeum limonis,* is more fragrant and valuable if obtained by expression than by distillation. Use the dried peel in incenses.

Lemon Balm (*Melissa officinalis*)

Folk Names: Sweet balm, honey plants, honey leaf. *See Balm.*

Lemongrass (*Cymbopogon citratus*)

Folk Names: Sweet rush

Gender: Hot

Planet: Sun

Element: Fire

Associated Deities: Ra, Osiris, Horus, Apollo, Bast, Sekhmet, Lugh, Bel, Adonis

Part Used: Leaves

Basic Powers: Attraction, love

Specific Uses: East Indian grass. Both grasses contain citral, an essential oil used in perfumery. Its crushed foliage smells like lemon. *See also Citronella.*

Lemon Verbena (*Lippia citriodora*)

Folk Names: Yerba Louisa, cedron, kunth

Gender: Cold

Planet: Venus

Element: Air

Associated Deities: Isis Osiris, Juno, Jupiter, Hera, Zeus, Odin

Part Used: Herb

Basic Powers: Protection, love

Specific Uses: Wear to make oneself attractive to the opposite sex. It is a strengthening herb often added to charms to add extra power. This is a tender plant that needs affection. Leaves can be substituted for lemon or mint in poultry, fish, and stuffing recipes.

Lettuce, Wild (*Lactuca virosa*)

Folk Names: Lettuce opium, green endive, acrid lettuce

Gender: Cold

Planet: Moon

Element: Water

Associated Deities: Isis, Khonsu, Kuan Yin, Neith, Diana, Hecate, Selene, Luna, Morrighan

Parts Used: Juice, leaves

Basic Powers: Psychic vision, prophecy, divination

Specific Uses: Hypnotic, narcotic, sedative; not safe unless you are a qualified herbalist. It was used as a tincture or smoked. Produces a dream or trance state. Enhances the vividness of dreams.

Licorice (*Glycyrrhiza glabra*)

Folk Names: Licorice root, sweet licorice, sweet wood

Gender: Cold

Planet: Mercury

Element: Earth/Air

Associated Deities: Mercury, Hermes, Thoth, Anubis, Maat, Odin, Oghma

Part Used: Root

Basic Powers: Protection, cursing, prophetic dreams

Specific Uses: In teas. Do NOT use on anyone with blood pressure problems.

Life Everlasting (*Antennaria margaritaceum*)

Folk Names: American everlasting, cudweed, pearl-flower

Gender: Cold

Planet: Venus

Element: Earth/Air

Associated Deities: Kuan Yin, Venus, Aphrodite, Hathor, Freyja, Brigid

Parts Used: Leaves, flowers, stalks

Basic Powers: Love, beauty, creativity

Specific Uses: Use in a poultice for sprains and bruises.

Lily of the Valley (*Convallaria magalis*)

Folk Names: May lily, May bells

Gender: Cold

Planet: Mercury

Element: Earth/Air

Associated Deities: Hermes, Thoth, Maat

Parts Used: Flowers. POISONOUS.

Basic Powers: Knowledge, peace

Specific Uses: A water distilled from the flowers called *aqua aurea* ("golden water"), was once thought to possess marvelous virtues to strengthen the memory and brain, and to comfort the heart. Legend says that it grows where the blood of a dragon had been spilled. Also used in perfumery.

Linden (*Tilia* spp.)

Folk Names: Lime tree, basswood, spoonwood, wicopy

Gender: Hot

Planet: Jupiter, sometimes Mercury

Element: Fire

Associated Deities: Brigid, Jupiter

Parts Used: Flowers, leaves, bark

Basic Powers: Love, luck

Specific Uses: A symbol of love and passion. It may have been the ruler of Summer Solstice in lowland areas where heather does not grow. Often used in love incense and with lavender in sleep pillows.

Loosestrife, Purple (*Lythrum salicaria*)

Folk Names: Willow-herb, rainbow weed, long purples

Gender: Cold

Planet: Moon

Element: Water

Associated Deities: Isis, Khonsu, Morrighan, Hecate

Part Used: Herb

Basic Powers: Peace, harmony

Specific Uses: This is an herb of peace, used in incense and sachets. Strewn about the house, it restores harmony.

Lotus (*Nymphaea odorata, N. lotus, Zizyphus lotus*)

Folk Names: Water lily, white pond lily, water cabbage, cow cabbage

Gender: Cold

Planet: Moon

Element: Water

Associated Deities: Isis, Khensu, Hecate, Neith, Selene

Parts Used: Rootstock, flowers. Root is poisonous.

Basic Powers: Fertility, visions, magick

Specific Uses: Revered by the Egyptians; represents the
   goddess Isis and human fertility. Flowers are used in
   perfumery.

Low John: *See Galangal.*

Lovage (*Levisticum officinale*)

Folk Names: Love root, lavose, sea parsley, Itlian
   parsley, loving herbs, love parsley, lubestico,
   Levistticum, Chinese lovage

Gender: Hot

Planet: Sun

Element: Water

Associated Deities: Isis, Diana, Brigid

Part Used: Root

Basic Powers: Love, purification

Specific Uses: Soaking a root in the bath refreshes one
   psychically and makes one more attractive to the
   opposite sex. Carry as a love attractor.

Lucky Hand: *See Satyrion* and *Ferns.*

Lungwort (*Sticta pulmonaria*)

Folk Names: Jerusalem cowslip, oak lungs, lung moss,
   spotted comfrey, Jerusalem sage, Adam and Eve

Gender: Hot

Planet: Jupiter

Element: Fire

Associated Deities: Jupiter, Zeus, Amun, Don, the
Dagda, Thor

Parts Used: Leaves, flowering herb

Basic Powers: Protection, uncrossing

Specific Uses: A member of the borage family, so it can
be used in much the same way.

Mace: *See Nutmeg.*

Mandrake (*Mandragora officinarum*, *Atropa mandragora*)

Folk Names: Mandragora, brain thief, Manniken,
wild lemon, raccoon berry, herb of Circe, Baaras,
womandrake

Gender: Hot

Planet: Mercury

Element: Earth

Associated Deities: Hecate, Hathor, Circe

Part Used: Root. POISONOUS.

Basic Powers: Protection, fertility

Specific Uses: The object of many strange beliefs, this
herb was considered very magickal. However, it is
poisonous. As the true mandrake is extremely rare,

the roots of the bryony or ash are good substitutes. In America, the May apple (*Podophyllum peltatum*) is considered a fair replacement. When available whole, both types of mandrake are placed on altars as protective devices. Traditionally the root was carved to resemble a human even more than it naturally does; it is used in image magick to avert misfortune and bring prosperity and happiness.

Marigold (*Calendula officinalis*)

Folk Names: Calendula, summer's bride, husbandman's dial, oligold, Marybud, marybud, marigold, bride of the Sun, pot marigold, spousa solis, golds, ruddes

Gender: Hot

Planet: Sun

Element: Fire

Associated Deities: Apollo, Ra, Thoth, Morrigan, Selene, Luna

Part Used: Flowers

Basic Powers: Love, clairvoyance, healing

Specific Uses: One of the ingredients in potions to see fairies. The ancients believed that it should be picked when the Moon was in Virgo, and it would give the wearer a vision of anyone who has robbed him/her. The petals are used in potpourris for color.

Sometimes it is added to love sachets. Place the flower beneath the head at night to have clairvoyant dreams.

Marjoram (*Origanum majorana*)

Folk Names: Joy of the mountains, marjorlaine, wintersweet, sweet marjoram, knotted marjoram, pot marjoram, mountain mint

Gender: Hot

Planet: Mercury

Element: Air

Associated Deities: Venus, Aphrodite

Parts Used: Herb

Basic Powers: Protection, love

Specific Uses: Add to all love charms. Put small pieces in every room of the house for protection. This should be changed every month. Make an infusion of marjoram, rosemary, and mint; sprinkle the house for protective vibrations; also used to cleanse objects.

Mastic (*Pistacia lentiscus*)

Folk Names: Masticke, gum mastic

Gender: Hot

Planet: Sun

Element: Fire

Associated Deities: Apollo, Ra, Horus, Bast, Sekhmet

Part Used: Gum

Basic Powers: Clairvoyance, manifestation

Specific Uses: Burn to help gain the Second Sight. It is most frequently used in incense.

Meadowsweet (*Filipendula ulmaria* or *Spirea ulmaris*)

Folk Names: Little queen, queen of the meadow, bridewort, gravel root, trumpet weed, steeplebush, meadsweet, dollor, meadow wort

Gender: Hot

Planet: Jupiter

Element: Water

Associated Deities: Jupiter, Zeus, the Dagda, Thor, Diana, Selene

Part used: Herb

Basic Power: Love

Specific Uses: One of the three most sacred herbs to the Druids: meadowsweet, vervain, and wild mint. Strewn around ritual circles for blessings. Add to love charms and sachets.

Melilot (*Melilotus officinalis*, *M. albar*, *M. arvensis*)

Folk Names: Sweet clover, king's clover, hart's true

Gender: Cold

Planet: Mercury

Element: Earth/Air

Associated Deities: Hermes, Thoth, Anubis, Odin, Maat

Parts Used: Herb

Basic Powers: Intellect, eloquence, creativity

Specific Uses: Its sweet odor increases when dried. Put in potpourris, sweet bags, and perfumes.

Milfoil *See Yarrow.*

Specific Uses: This herb is considered to be highly spiritual in nature.

Mimosa *See Acacia.*

Mistletoe (*Viscum album*)

Folk Names: Birdlime, donnerbesen, all heal, devil's fuge, thunderbesom, golden bough, European mistletoe

Gender: Hot

Planet: Sun

Element: Air

Associated Deities: Horus, Ra, Apollo, Bast, Bel

Part Used: Herb

Basic Powers: Protection, love

Specific Uses: The Gallic Druids called this the most important "tree" of all; it was cut from an oak with a golden sickle. In the Druidic language, this herb means "all-heal" and rules the Winter Solstice. The berries are poisonous if consumed. Pick on Summer Solstice and wear as a protective amulet or to help conceive.

Moonwort (*Botrychium lunaria*)

Folk Name: Martagon

Gender: Cold

Planet: Moon

Element: Water

Associated Deities: Isis, Khonsu, Neith, Hecate, Morrigan

Part Used: Crescent-shaped leaflets and fronds

Basic Powers: Love, divination, magick

Specific Uses: To open a lock or break chains, place in it a piece of moonwort. Similar to adder's tongue.

Motherwort (*Leonurus cardiaca*)

Folk Names: Lion's ear, lion's tail, throwwort

Gender: Cold

Planet: Venus

Element: Earth/Air

Associated Deities: Venus, Aphrodite, Hathor, Astarte, Freyja

Parts Used: Flowering tops, leaves

Basic Power: Protection

Specific Uses: Said to be powerful against evil spirits, so it was used to stuff pillows and strewn around the house.

Mugwort (*Artemisia vulgaris*, genus *Artemisia*)

Folk Names: Naughty man, old man, old uncle Harry, artermisia, Artemis herb, muggons, sailor's tobacco, felon herb, motherwort

Gender: Cold

Planet: Venus

Element: Air

Associated Deities: Artemis, Diana, Luna, Selene

Part Used: Herb

Specific Uses: Make a simple infusion and drink it to induce clairvoyance. Rub the fresh leaves on magick mirrors and crystal balls to strengthen their powers. Add to scrying, clairvoyance, and divination incenses. Sacred to Artemis and the moon. Tradition says that the odor is supposed to open the third eye and heighten awareness. Gather on Summer Solstice to protect against disease and misfortune.

Pick before sunrise during the waxing Moon, preferably from a plant that leans north. The plant's powers are strongest when picked on the full Moon. One of the world's most used medicines.

Mulberry (*Morus nigra, M. rubra*)

Folk Names: Black mulberry, red mulberry

Gender: Cold

Planet: Mercury

Element: Earth/Air

Associated Deities: Minerva, Mercury, Thoth, Maat, Athena, Hermes

Parts Used: Fruit, bark

Basic Power: Knowledge

Specific Uses: Use in incense or sachet bags, as this herb is sacred to Minerva especially and is a symbol of wisdom.

Mullein (*Verbascum thapsus*)

Folk Names: Hag's tapers, torches, clot, feltwort, doffle, candlewick plant, Aaron's rod, Peter's staff, lady's foxglove, velvet plant, Jupiter's staff, shepherd's herb, old man's fennel, velvetback, flannet plant, hedge taper, blanket leaf

Gender: Cold

Planet: Saturn

Element: Fire

Associated Deities: Saturn, Kronos, Jupiter, Odin

Part Used: Herb

Basic Power: Protection

Specific Uses: Said to drive away evil spirits and protects against attacking magick. Carry to keep away wild animals and instill courage. The powdered leaves are also known as "graveyard dust" and are acceptable as a substitute when such is called for in old recipes.

Mustard (*Brassica nigra, Sinapis nigra*)

Folk Names: White mustard, black mustard, field mustard, cole see, common hedge, flixweed, treacle hedge, mithridate

Gender: Hot

Planet: Mars

Element: Earth/Fire

Associated Deities: Asclepius, Mars

Part Used: Seeds

Basic Power: Healing

Specific Uses: Diuretic, emetic; plaster for bronchitis and pneumonia.

Myrrh (*Commiphora myrrha*)

Folk Names: Karan, mirra balsom, odendron, gum myrrh

Gender: Hot

Planet: Sun

Element: Water

Associated Deities: Isis, Adonis, Ra, Marian

Part Used: Resin

Basic Powers: Protection, purification

Specific Uses: Burn to purify and protect an area or person. The smoke is used to consecrate and bless objects, such as charm bags and ritual tools. It was used in sacred ointments and anointing oils for purification of women; known also as Tears of the Goddess. It is an ingredient in Holy Oil, Kyphi, and many incenses used for fumigations and exorcism. Myrrh oil can be burned in ritual lamps; it is also a fixative in potpourris and perfumes. Was burned in ancient Egyptian temples of Isis.

Myrtle (*Myrtus communis, Myrica cerifera*)

Folk Names: Candleberry, waxberry, bayberry tree, wax myrtle

Gender: Cold

Planet: Venus

Element: Water

Associated Deities: Artemis, Aphrodite, Hathor, Astarte, Ashtoreth, Venus, Marian

Parts Used: Herb

Basic Powers: Love, fertility

Specific Uses: One of the strictly love herbs. Add to all love sachets. Carry the wood to preserve youthfulness. This tree is the Greek equivalent of the elder and is a symbol of justice. Add to incenses made for Aphrodite and the sea.

Narcissus (*Narcissus tazetta*)

Folk Names: Daffodil, lent lily, jonquil

Gender: Cold

Planet: Venus

Element: Earth/Air

Associated Deity: Persephone

Part Used: Flowers

Basic Powers: Visions, trance, divination

Specific Uses: Symbolizes death and other Underworld deities. As a narcotic and anciently considered poisonous, smelling too much of its odor would drive one mad. The daffodil is *Narcissus pseudo-narcissus*, and its flowers add to potpourri for color; it is also infused in massage oils. Narcissus oil used in perfumery is from the jonquil (*N. jonuilla*) and the Campernella (*N. odorus*).

Nasturtium (*Nasturtium officinale, Tropaeolum majus*)

Folk Name: Indian cress, watercress

Gender: Cold

Planet: Saturn

Element: Earth

Associated Deities: Saturn, Kronos, Nephthys, Isis, Demeter, Ceres, Nut, Cerridwen, Danu, Hecate

Parts Used: Flowers, leaves, seeds

Basic Powers: Protection, uncrossing, reincarnation, study, knowledge

Specific Uses: Seeds used in incenses for psychic sight.

Nettle (*Urtica dioica*-greater or *U. urens*-lesser)

Folk Names: common nettle, stinging nettle

Gender: Hot

Planet: Mars

Element: Fire

Associated Deities: Osiris, Isis, Odin

Part Used: Herb

Basic Powers: Protection, exorcism

Specific Uses: Stuff a poppet with nettles to remove a curse and send it back to the sender. Write the name of the sender on the poppet and then bury or burn it. Can be added to protection sachets, and burned during exorcism ceremonies. The stinging quality disappears when dried.

Nightshade, Deadly: (*Atropa belladonna*). *See Belladonna.*

Gender: Cold

Planet: Saturn

Element: Earth

Associated Deities: Hecate, Saturn

Part Used: Herb. POISONOUS.

Basic Powers: Knowledge, binding

Specific Uses: An ingredient in incense to promote psychic vision and astral travel, it was never used internally.

Nutmeg (*Myristica fragrans*)

Folk Names: Mace, arillus myristicae, macia

Gender: Hot

Planet: Jupiter, sometimes Mercury

Element: Air

Associated Deities: Thoth, Hermes, Jupiter, Odin, Osiris

Part Used: Seed

Basic Power: Clairvoyance

Specific Uses: Carry to strengthen your clairvoyant skills and ward off rheumatism. Add sparingly to divinatory incenses. The dried kernel of the seed is called nutmeg, while the dried arils of the seed are called mace. Both are used in potpourris and perfumes for their aromas. In large doses they are narcotic. Hollowed-out nutmegs filled with mercury and carved are considered good luck charms. Oil of nutmeg can be rubbed lightly on the temples to induce sleep and aid meditation.

Nuts and Cones: (*var.*)

Basic Powers: Fertility, healing

Specific Uses: All nuts and cones are said to be steeped in magick. Add to charm bags.

Oak (*Quercus rober, Q. alba*)

Folk Names: Tanner's bark, white oak

Gender: Hot

Planet: Sun, sometimes Jupiter

Element: Fire

Associated Deities: the Dagda, Dianus, Jupiter, Zeus, Thor, Llyr, Llud, Herne, Hercules, Cerridwen, Cernunnos, Janus, Rhea, Cybele

Part Used: Seed, bark, leaves

Basic Powers: Fertility, protection, longevity

Specific Uses: A holy tree of the Druids, whose name comes from the word for oak, *Duir*. It was the king of trees in the sacred groves; they made magickal wands from its wood. The sacred fires in the Roman Vestal temples were of oak. It symbolizes royalty, endurance, triumph, and the power of thunderstorms. Dryads are the spirits who live in oak trees and gave inspiration to the Druids. Oak galls were also called "serpent eggs" and were used in Druidic charms. The acorn is carried to preserve youthfulness and ward off illnesses. Hang in windows to protect the house.

Oak, Holly (*Quercus ilex*, *Q. coccinea*, *Q. coccifera*)

Folk names: Red oak, scarlet oak, Kerm oak, bloody oak

Gender: Hot

Planet: Mars

Element: Fire

Associated Deities: Mars, the Furies, Ares, Tiw, Thor

Part Used: Wood

Basic Powers: Protection, energy

Specific Uses: An evergreen, it rules the waning part of the year while the common oak rules the waxing part.

Oakmoss (*Evernia prunastri*)

Gender: Cold

Planet: Mercury

Element: Air

Associated Deities: Hermes, Thoth

Part Used: Herb

Basic Powers: Intellect, conjurations

Specific Uses: It is a lichen that grows on oak trees and is used in perfumery as a fixative to assist in the uniform evaporation of the other ingredients. Also was the base for fine cosmetic body powder known as Chypre, whose use goes as far back as ancient Egypt.

Olibanum: *See Frankincense.*

Olive (*Olea europaea*)

Gender: Hot

Planet: Jupiter

Element: Fire/Water

Associated Deities: Apollo, Helios, Athena

Parts Used: Leaves, bark, fruit, wood

Basic Powers: Peace, luck, honor

Specific Uses: Symbolizes fruitfulness, peace, and happiness; the oil represents goodness and purity. Olive oil was burned in sacred temple lamps. Associated with the Spring Equinox where the boughs were used in Greek spring festivals. Sacred to the young Sun. Its wood was used for statues of deities. Olympic game victors were crowned with olive wreaths.

Onion (*Allium cepa*)

Folk Names: Yn-leac, Oingnum, Unyoun, Onyoun

Gender: Hot

Planet: Mars

Element: Fire

Associated Deities: Luna, Hecate, Thor, Odin, Isis, Horus

Parts Used: Bulb, flowers

Basic Powers: Protection, purification, exorcism, healing

Specific Uses: Place onion halves in rooms to absorb illnesses and diseases then throw away the onions without touching them. Rub a ritual knife's blade with onion to cleanse it. Sacred to the moon and used in lunar rites. Also used in protective spells along with garlic. Was a symbol of eternity to ancient Egyptians.

Raw onion is an antidote to an external insect bite; it can also be used on badly bruised or sprained body parts. By breaking up fluid congestion, such as in bruising and swelling, it is also an anti-inflammatory that draws out lymph fluids. It also cleanses the blood and lowers high blood pressure.

Onycha (*Unguis odoratus, Cistus creticus, C. landaniferus*).
See also Rock Rose.

    Folk Names: Labdanum, rock rose, nail, claw

    Gender: Hot

    Planet: Sun

    Element: Fire

    Associated Deities: Horus, Ra, Apollo, Adonis, Lugh

    Parts Used: Shell, flower

    Basic Powers: Success, prosperity

    Specific Uses: Its name means "nail" or "claw"; as
       an ingredient of the holy incense of Exodus, it
       meant the horny operculum, or shell, of a species
       of shellfish, *U. aromatic* or *U. oderatus*, found in
       the spikenard lakes of India. Others claim that it is
       a rock rose, *Cistua landaniferus*, which produces a
       gum called labdanum.

Opoponax (*Opopanax chironium*)

    Folk Name: Pastinaca opoponax

    Gender: Hot

    Planet: Sun

    Element: Water

    Associated Deities: Isis, Adonis, Ra

    Part Used: Juice

    Basic Powers: Protection, purification

Specific Uses: The concrete juice from the base of the stem is used as a fixative in perfumery and fragrant dry mixtures. An inferior quality of myrrh is also called opoponax.

Orange (Sweet: *Citrus sinensis* or *C. Aurantium var. dulcis*; Bitter: *Citrus vulgaris var. bigaradis* or *C. aurantium var. amara*).

Folk Name: Love fruit

Gender: Hot

Planet: Sun

Element: Water

Associated Deities: Venus, Aphrodite, Adonis, Apollo

Parts Used: Rind, fruit, flowers

Basic Powers: Love

Specific Uses: Add dried peel to love sachets and charm bags. Add the fresh or dried blossoms to an attract love bath. Oil of petit grain, also known as neroli, is made from the leaves and young shoots of the bitter oranges; its scent is said to sharpen awareness. Neroli is also used in perfumery, as are the blossoms and peel. Bitter oranges are made into pomanders as Winter Solstice gifts. Neroli oil has a hypnotic scent that helps with sleep and nervous conditions. The flowers can be put in sleep pillows.

Orris (*Iris* var. *florentina*, *I. germanica*, or *I. pallid*)

Folk Names: Queen Elizabeth root, Florentine iris, iris, yellow flag

Gender: Cold

Planet: Venus, sometimes the Sun and Jupiter

Element: Water

Associated Deities: Iris, Juno, Venus

Part Used: Root

Basic Power: Love

Specific Uses: Use in small quantities in love incenses. Add powdered orris to love sachets and baths. Add to lavender and rosebuds to make sachets. The root is used in perfumery, for its violet-like odor and its power of strengthening the scent of other ingredients. It is a symbol of power and majesty; the Egyptians placed the plant on the scepters of pharaohs. The dried root develops its best scent after it has been stored for two years or more.

Palm, Date (*Phoenix dactylifera*)

Gender: Hot

Planet: Jupiter

Element: Water

Associated Deities: Ishtar, Ashtoreth, Isis, Venus, Astarte, Aphrodite, all mother goddesses

Parts Used: Bark, leaves, wood

Basic Powers: Love, protection

Specific Uses: The birth tree and symbol of motherhood in the more southerly latitudes. It is a water tree, as it grows by the sea.

Paprika (*Capsicum annum*). *See Pepper.*

Parsley (*Carum petroselinum*; *Petroselinum sativum*)

Folk Names: Garden parsley, rock parsley

Gender: Cold

Planet: Mercury

Element: Earth/Air

Associated Deities: Mercury, Hermes, Thoth, Anubis, Maat, Odin, Oghma

Parts Used: Root, seeds, plant

Basic Powers: Clairvoyance, scrying, prediction, creativity

Specific Uses: Seeds and root are stronger in incenses than the leaf. Although a symbol of death in ancient Greece and Rome, it was awarded as prizes in public games.

Patchouli (*Pogostemon cablin, P. patchouli*)

Folk Name: Pucha-pot

Gender: Hot

Planet: Sun, sometimes Mars

Element: Earth

Associated Deities: Ishtar, Ashtoreth, Isis, Venus, Aphrodite

Part used: Herb, oil

Basic Powers: Passion, love

Specific Uses: Usually used in oil form. Wear alone or with other love herbs. Also burned in clairvoyance and divination incenses. Improves as it ages. Used also as a fixative and blender.

Pennyroyal (*Mentha pulegium*)

Folk Names: Squaw mint, run-by-the-ground, lurk-in-the-ditch, pudding grass, piliolerian, tickweed, mosquito plant

Gender: Cold

Planet: Venus

Element: Earth

Associated Deities: Hecate, Cerridwen

Part Used: Herb

Basic Powers: Protection, exorcism, healing

Specific Uses: Add to summer incenses to protect and exorcise. A very mild tea from the leaves can sometimes help migraine headaches. Its odor also repels fleas.

Peony (*Paeonia officinalis*)

Gender: Hot

Planet: Sun

Element: Fire

Associated Deities: Paeon, Apollo

Parts Used: Herb

Basic Powers: Protection, exorcism

Specific Uses: Believed to guard the home from storms and demons. The plant was thought to have emanated from the moon as it shines during the night and drives away evil spirits. Burn the seeds during exorcism rituals or to stop storms.

Pepper, Black (*Piper nigrum*)

Gender: Hot

Planet: Mars

Element: Fire/Water

Associated Deities: Mars, Ares, Horus, Tiw

Part Used: Dried unripe fruit

Basic Powers: Cursing, control, protection, exorcism

Specific Uses: Do not remain in an enclosed place if burning this in incense.

Pepper, Red (*Capsicum* spp.)

Folk Names: Cayenne, red pepper, capsicum

Gender: Hot

Planet: Mars

Element: Fire

Associated Deities: Ares, Thor, Anubis, Maat

Part Used: Fruit

Basic Power: Protection

Specific Uses: Use in charm bags and amulets for protection. If burned, mix with others, such as rosemary and dill; this is used to fumigate and exorcise a place. Since the smoke is quite stinging to the eyes and skin, I do not recommend this be done within an enclosed space; the smoke is also harmful to pets.

Peppermint (*Mentha piperita*)

Folk Names: Lammint, brandy mint

Gender: Cold

Planet: Venus, sometimes the Moon

Element: Air

Associated Deities: Apollo, Luna, Aphrodite, Isis

Part Used: Herb

Basic Powers: Healing, purification

Specific Uses: Add to healing incenses and charms. Also burn the leaves to cleanse the house in winter. Drink peppermint tea when you have a cold or sinus problems. Peppermint oil or leaf made into a tea is relaxing and soothing, and it also relieves congestion and helps with circulation. Headaches sometimes are helped by putting a drop of oil on the temples. It also works for motion sickness, upset stomach, chest congestion, colic, and as a tea is a stimulating hair rinse.

Periwinkle, Greater (*Vinca major* or *V. pervinca*)

Gender: Cold

Planet: Venus

Element: Water

Associated Deities: Aphrodite, Isis, Adonis, Luna, Astarte

Part Used: Flowers

Basic Powers: Protection, love

Specific Uses: This was a favorite flower of the "wise folk" for making charms and love philters, and it was believed to protect from evil spirits, snakes, wild beasts, poison, possession, evil magick, hatred, and terror when hung in the doorway. Also brings prosperity. Must be picked when the Moon is nine, eleven, thirteen, thirty, or one night old. The Germans decorated tombs with it for immortality.

Peyote (*Anhalonium lewinii* or *A. williamsii*)

Folk Names: Devil's root, dumpling cactus, mescal button, pellote, sacred mushroom

Gender: Cold

Planet: Mercury

Element: Air

Associated Deities: Hermes, Thoth, Maat, Anubis

Part Used: Plant. DANGEROUS.

Basic Powers: Visions.

Specific Uses: The tops, consisting of blunt leaves around a tuft of short, pale yellow hairs, are used by some Native American tribes for producing hallucinogenic visions during religious ceremonies.

Pimpernel (*Pimpinella magna*)

Folk Names: Greater Pimpernell, Pimpinella

Gender: Hot

Element: Air

Part Used: Herb

Basic Power: Protection

Specific Uses: Good to protect the home and to guard against illness.

Pine (*Pinus* spp.)

Gender: Hot

Planet: Mars

Element: Earth

Associated Deities: Cybele, Venus, Attis, Pan, Dionysus, the Horned God

Parts Used: Cone, nuts, needles

Basic Powers: Fertility, purification

Specific Uses: Burn the crushed and dried needles in the winter to purify the home; mix equal parts juniper and cedar. The cones and nuts can be carried or hung as fertility charms. If performing magick outside, sweep the area with a pine branch. Add crushed needles to a bath sachet for a good winter magickal cleansing. One of the seven chieftain trees of the Irish. Also put in sleep and dream pillows.

Pomegranate (*Pumica granatum*)

Folk Names: Melogranato, Cortezade Granada

Gender: Cold

Planet: Venus

Element: Earth/Air

Associated Deities: Adonis, the Great Mother, Astarte, Aphrodite

Parts Used: Root, bark, fruits, rind of the fruit, flowers

Basic Powers: Fertility, love

Specific Uses: Symbol of fertility and parthenogenesis; it was the only fruit allowed in the Hebrew Holiest of Holies. It was the mystic fruit of the Eleusinian mysteries and was also revered by the ancient Egyptians. Associated with the Winter Solstice.

Poplar (*Populus* spp.)

Folk Names: Quaking aspen, trembling poplar, balm of Gilead

Gender: Cold

Planet: Saturn

Element: Earth

Associated Deities: Saturn, Nephthys, Isis, Cerridwen, Danu, Hecate

Parts Used: Bark, buds

Basic Powers: Protection, knowledge, healing

Specific Uses: Poplar and Black Poplar are known in the US, especially the South, as Balm of Gilead. The buds of tacamahac (*Populus balsamifera*) can be used in place of balm of Gilead buds. White poplar is the same as aspen. *P. candicans* and its buds are also known as balm of Gilead. Black Poplar is the tree of heroes and a funeral tree sacred to Mother Earth.

Like the willow and aspen, poplar bark is useful as an anti-inflammatory and analgesic.

The buds of black poplar are called gillie buds. The buds are boiled with a small covering amount of olive oil for ten to fifteen minutes; strain out the buds. Add a small amount of beeswax to the oil to slightly thicken. Cap tightly in a bottle. Rub on joints for arthritis. Gather and dry buds in the spring for use.

Poppy (*Papaver* spp., *P. somniferum*).

Folk Names: Head waak, blind buff, laudanum, opium poppy

Gender: Cold

Planet: Moon

Element: Water

Associated Deities: Hypnos, Somnos, Ceres

Parts Used: Seeds, dried seed pods. DANGEROUS.

Basic Powers: Fertility, prosperity

Specific Uses: The tincture of the capsule is known as laudanum. The capsule and flowers contain opium, a strong, addictive hypnotic and sedative; also a pain reliever and antispasmodic. Overdoses can be fatal. It is best to use it in charm bags for prosperity and abundance.

Primrose (*Primula vulgaris*)

Folk Names: Butter rose, English cowslip, password

Gender: Cold

Planet: Venus

Element: Fire

Associated Deities: Freyja

Part Used: Flowers

Basic Power: Protection

Specific Uses: Plant in the garden to protect, especially the blue and red primroses. Especially powerful planted in pots sitting on the stoop and back porches.

Quince (*Pyrus cydonia, Cydonia vulgaris, C. oblonga*)

Folk Name: Coyne

Gender: Cold

Planet: Saturn

Element: Earth

Associated Deities: Venus, Aphrodite

Parts Used: Seeds, fruit

Basic Powers: Love

Specific Uses: Sacred to the Goddess in her Venus/ Aphrodite aspect. This is the apple of the Greeks and Hebrews, as well as in other ancient myths. A symbol of love and happiness, this fruit also wards against the evil eye.

Ranunculus: (*Ranunculus bulbosus, Ranunculus acis*)

    Folk Names: Buttercup, blisterweed, crowfoot, frogwort, king's cup, pilewort. St. Anthony's turnip, goldcup

    Gender: Cold

    Planet: Moon

    Element: Water

    Associated Deities: Isis Khensu, Neith, Kuan Yin, Diana, Hecate, Selene, Luna, Morrighan

    Part Used: Plant

    Basic Powers: Prophecy, divination, scrying

    Specific Uses: Add to incenses and sachets.

Reed (*Phragmites maxima*)

    Gender: Cold

    Planet: Saturn

    Element: Earth

    Associated Deities: Osiris, Thoth, Hermes, Maat, Isis, Cerridwen

    Part Used: Herb

    Basic Powers: Eloquence, knowledge

    Specific Uses: Irish poets reckoned this a tree. Reeds were used for arrow shafts and royal scepters, such as Egyptian pharaohs, for example.

Rock Rose (*Cistus creticus*). *See also Onycha.*

Folk Names: European rock rose, labdanum, onycha, frostwort

Gender: Hot

Planet: Sun

Element: Fire

Associated Deities: Horus, Ra, Apollo, Adonis, Lugh

Part used: Gum resin

Basic Powers: Success, prosperity

Specific Uses: Yields the gum resin ladanum or labdanum, a natural exudation. An oil with the odor of ambergris has been obtained from this resin. Labdanum is found in masses weighing up to several pounds enclosed in plant bladders. It softens in the hand when broken, becoming adhesive and balsamic; it burns with a clear flame. *Cistus ledon* and *C. laurifolius* are said to yield the same substance.

Rose (*Rosa* spp.)

Gender: Cold

Planet: Venus

Element: Water

Associated Deities: Venus, Hulda, Demeter, Isis, Eros, Cupid, Adonis

Part Used: Flowers

Basic Powers: Love, fertility, clairvoyance

Specific Uses: Legend says this plant sprang from the
blood of Adonis. Originated in northern Persia;
there are more than ten thousand varieties and
colors. Also considered the master herb of love,
planting roses in your yard is said to bring good luck
and good fortune.

Heavily used in perfumery, potpourris, strewing,
incense making, and scented beads. The old custom
of suspending a rose over the dinner table was a sign
that all confidences were to be held sacred ("under
the rose," or *sub rosa).* The most fragrant species
for perfumery are *Rose centifolia* (cabbage rose),
Rosa damascena (damask rose), and *Rosa indica*
(Tea rose). For medicinal use and sometimes for
potpourris, *Rosa gallica* (provins rose) is used. Wash
your hands with rose water before mixing up love
mixtures. Drink a tisane of rose petals to produce
clairvoyant dreams. Burn the petals in the bedroom
prior to sleep and have a completely refreshing night.
The petals can be added to healing incenses and
sachets.

Rosemary (*Rosmarinus officinalis*)

Folk Names: Dew of the sea, incensier, sea dew, ros maris, Rosmarine, rosemarie, guardrobe

Gender: Hot

Planet: Sun, sometimes the moon

Element: Fire

Associated Deities: Apollo, Bast, Horus, Ra, Sekhmet

Part Used: Herb

Basic Powers: Purfication, love, intellect, protection

Specific Uses: Much esteemed by the ancients, and used as religious incense and in spells. It is powerful protection from evil influences in general. Anoint your doors and windowsills with rosemary oil to exorcise and protect your home, and burn incense for cleansing exorcisms and purification. Add to all purification bath sachets, love incenses, exorcism mixtures, and protection incenses. Make a tisane to cleanse the hands before working magick. Rosemary does not yield its virtues to water, so boil the leaves in white wine. It has connections with the sea and is used in all sea rituals, as well as in sachets designed to ensure a safe passage on water. It is used in perfumery and potpourris for its lovely fragrance. Also used in love potions and psychic oils. Was once used as a decoration for Winter Solstice festivals.

Drink rosemary tea just before a test or exam to ensure that the mind is alert. Burn rosemary and juniper as a healing and recuperation incense.

Rowan (*Fraxinus aucuparia, Pyrus aucuparia, Sorbus aucuparis*)

Folk Names: Mountain ash, witchwood, quickbane, wild ash, witchen, witchbane, wicken tree, wiky, wiggy, roynetree, whitty, wiggin ran tree, roden-quicken-royan, sorb apple, roden-quicken, delight of the eye

Gender: Hot

Planet: Sun

Element: Fire

Associated Deities: Thor, Gauri, Yao-Shih, Brigid, the Muses

Parts Used: Wood, twigs, seeds. Seeds are POISONOUS.

Basic Powers: Protection, healing

Specific Uses: Use the rowan branches in divining for water, as is often done with witch hazel wood. Was believed to be protection against lightning. Magickal wands are made from this wood; so are rods, amulets, and charms. Rowan wands are for knowledge, finding metal, and divination in general.

As an oracular tree, it often grows near stone circles. Sacred to Brigid and the Muses as it symbolizes divination and inspiration; also all the fire goddesses; a fire tree because of its red berries, which are considered very magickal. The Druids made fires of rowan wood and chanted incantations over them before battle, to summon spirits to their aid. They also used rowan wattles spread on a newly flayed bull's hide as a last resort to force spirits to answer difficult questions. The seeds are poisonous, as they contain cyanide.

Rue (*Ruta graveolens*)

Folk Names: Rua, bashoush, German rue, garden rue, Rewe, hreow, herbygrass, herb of grace, mother of the herbs

Gender: Hot

Planet: Sun, sometimes Saturn

Element: Fire

Associated Deities: Diana, Aradia

Part Used: Herb

Basic Powers: Protection, intellect, exorcism, purification.

Specific Uses: Highly regarded in ancient times, almost as much as rosemary. Is an antidote against evil spells. Rue branches were used as sprinklers in rituals as they were symbols of purification. It is burned to ward off psychic attacks. Rue is added to health sachets and other charm bags to keep illness away. Add to exorcism incenses and purification sachets. It is good to use in spells of inertia to get something moving.

Saffron (*Crocus sativus*)

Folk Names: Autumn crocus, Spanish saffron, crocus

Gender: Hot

Planet: Sun, sometimes Jupiter

Element: Fire

Associated Deities: Apollo, Hermes, Brigid, the Muses

Part Used: Flowers

Basic Powers: Purification, clairvoyance, healing

Specific Uses: The flower stigmas and styles, called threads, produce a vivid yellow dye, are used in perfumery, and have medicinal uses. Gives off a distinctive, aromatic odor. This herb is so expensive, however, that dried marigold petals may be substituted for it in any spell.

Sage (*Salvia officinalis* varieties)

Folk Names: Garden sage, red sage, white sage

Gender: Hot

Planet: Jupiter

Element: Earth

Associated Deities: Jupiter, Zeus, Amun, Thor

Part Used: Herb

Basic Powers: Healing, prosperity, purification

Specific Uses: It is a symbol of immortality and wisdom; hang a branch over the door to absorb all ill fortune. Add to healing and prosperity sachets, incenses, and amulets. Harvest the leaves just before they flower in the early summer; dry in the shade. It works against strep, staph, *E. coli*, candida, and salmonella. Is a broad spectrum antibiotic, and has been use as medicine for at least two millennia in nearly every culture.

St. John's Wort (*Hypericum perforatum*)

Folk Names: Herba jon, John's wort, Frega daemonum, goat weed, tipton weed, amber, Klath weed

Gender: Hot

Planet: Sun, sometimes Mercury

Element: Fire

Associated Deities: Horus, Ra, Apollo, Bast, Sekhmet

Part Used: Herb

Basic Powers: Protection, exorcism

Specific Uses: Burn to banish and exorcise spirits.
Wear the herb to make you invincible in battles of all
kinds, and strengthen your own will.

Salt

While not an herb, salt is very important in many magickal
workings. Coarse-grained sea salt or Dead Sea Salt is
the best to use for rituals and spells as it has no additives
(usually anti-caking agents). Salt is a creature of the Earth,
and may be added with good effect to any incense of that
particular element, or a few grains to other types.

Sandalwood (*Santalum album*)

Folk Names: Santal, Sandal, white saunders, yellow
sandalwood

Gender: Cold

Planet: Moon (white and red), sometimes Mercury
(white), Venus (red)

Element: Air

Associated Deities: Isis, Selene, Morrigan, Venus,
Luna, Hermes, Thoth

Parts Used: Wood

Basic Powers: Protection, purification, healing

Specific Uses: Is sacred to Mercury and its wood is
used in incenses for occult knowledge. The scent

takes away irrational fears and anxieties and is rejuvenating and protective. An excellent all-purpose purification and anointing oil can be made by combining sandalwood and rose oils. Add this wood dust to healing incenses and burn as a good purifying agent in any room. Red sandalwood (*Pterocarpus santalinus* and *S. rubrun*) is a different tree, sacred to Venus.

Sanicle (*Sanicula europaea*)

Folk Names: European sanicle, wood sanicle, self-heal, poolroot, black snake root

Gender: Hot

Planet: Mars

Element: Fire/Water

Associated Deities: Mars, Ares, Horus, Tiw

Part Used: Leaves

Basic Powers: Protection, control, curing, exorcism

Santal: *See Saunders, Red; Sandalwood*

Sassafras (*Sassafras officinale*)

Folk Names: Saxifrax, cinnamon wood, ague tree

Gender: Cold

Planet: Moon

Element: Water

Associated Deities: Isis Khensu, Neith, Kuan Yin, Diana, Hecate, Selene, Luna, Morrigan

Part Used: Bark

Basic Powers: Healing, sexual attraction, control, dreams

Specific Uses: Within the last century, sassafras tea was still drunk for discomfort of women's menses.

Satyrion (*Orchis* spp.)

Folk Names: Orchid, satyr orchid

Gender: Cold

Planet: Venus

Element: Air

Associated Deities: Aphrodite, Astarte, Freyja, Hathor

Part Used: Root

Basic Power: Love

Specific Uses: Root is said to be a powerful aphrodisiac and ingredient of numerous love charms and philters. The name comes from the ancient belief that the root resembles the male sexual organ.

Saunders, Red (*Pterocarpus santalinus*)

Folk Names: Red sandalwood, ruby wood, red santal wood, sappan, lignum rubrum

Gender: Cold

Planet: Venus

Element: Air

Associated Deities: Isis, Selene, Kuan Yin, Venus, Luna, Morrighan, Thoth, Hermes

Parts Used: Wood

Basic Powers: Protection, purification, healing, love

Specific Uses: Used in incenses. Blood-red color with an interesting scent. *See Sandalwood.*

Savory, Summer (*Satureja hortensis*)

Folk Name: Beam herb

Gender: Cold

Planet: Venus

Element: Earth/Air

Associated Deities: Venus, Aphrodite, Hathor, Freyja, Kuan Yin, Brigid

Parts Used: Herb

Basic Powers: Love, sexual attraction, dreams, creativity

Specific Uses: Legends says that this was the herb loved by the satyrs. Slightly peppery taste and smell.

Savory, Winter (*Satureja montana*)

Basic Powers: Same as summer savory.

Scammony (*Convolvulus sepium*)

Folk Names: Greater bindweed root, hedge bindweed, devil's vine, hedge lily, lady's nightcap

Gender: Cold

Planet: Saturn

Element: Earth

Associated Deities: Saturn, Kronos

Parts Used: Resin, flowering plant, rootstock

Basic Powers: Harvests, success

Specific Use: Incenses only.

Silverweed (*Potentilla anserina*)

Folk Names: Prince's feathers, trailing tansy, goosewort, silvery cinquefoil, moor grass, wild agrimony.

Gender: Hot

Planet: Jupiter

Element: Fire/Water

Associated Deities: Jupiter, Zeus, Amun, Don, the Dagda, Thor

Part Used: Herb

Basic Powers: Success, prosperity

Specific Uses: Add to incenses and sachets.

Slippery Elm (*Ulmus fulva*)

Folk Names: Red elm, moose elm, Indian elm

Gender: Cold

Element: Earth

Associated Deities: Saturn, Isis, Hecate

Parts Used: Leaves, bark

Basic Power: Protection

Specific Uses: Burn and use in charm bags to stop others from gossiping about you or your friends.

Snapdragon (*Antirrhinum majus*)

Gender: Cold

Planet: Venus

Element: Fire

Associated Deities: Venus, Aphrodite, Hathor, Freyja

Parts Used: Flowers, leaves

Specific Uses: The flowers are a powerful antidote to black magick. Wear as a protective amulet, or put vases of flowers in the house if you feel threatened. Carry with you to see through other people's deceit. Also can be used to counteract charms and spells laid by others by adding to incenses and oil mixtures.

Solomon's Seal (*Polygonatum multiflorum* or *P. odoratum*)

Folk Names: Dropberry, sealwort, sealroot

Gender: Hot

Planet: Saturn

Element: Fire

Associated Deities: Kronos, Nephthys, Isis, Demeter, Cerridwen, Hecate

Parts Used: Leaves, roots

Basic Powers: Purification, protection

Specific Uses: Add to incenses and sachets to protect. Scatter to the four winds as an offering to the elementals. Also use in love charms, cleansing, and exorcism mixtures.

Southernwood (*Artemisia abrotanum*)

Folk Names: Old man, lad's love, boy's love, applering

Gender: Cold

Planet: Mercury, sometimes the moon

Element: Earth/Air

Associated Deities: Mercury, Hermes, Thoth, Anubis, Maat, Odin, Oghma

Part Used: Herb

Basic Powers: Clairvoyance, knowledge, magick

Specific Uses: Has an invigorating scent that overrides cooking and tobacco odors. The finely divided leaves with a lemon smell are considered a sexual stimulant.

Spearmint (*Mentha spicata, M. viridis*)

Folk Names: Garden mint, lamb mint, green spine, spice mint, our lady's mint, mackerel mint, brown mint

Gender: Cold

Planet: Venus

Element: Air

Associated Deities: Isis, Aphrodite, Venus, Freyja, Brigid

Part Used: Herb

Basic Powers: Healing, love

Specific Uses: Add to healing incenses and poppets, especially for curing lung diseases. A good addition to love mixtures and sachets; it is like peppermint but less powerful. A milder version of mint, it often works better for children.

Spikenard (*Nardostachys jatamansi*)

Folk Names: Sambal, nard, nardos, nardin

Gender: Cold

Planet: Venus

Element: Earth/Air

Associated Deities: Hathor, Venus, Freyja

Part Used: Flowers

Basic Powers: Love, creativity

Specific Uses: Used in incense and perfume oils. Very famous perfume of the East that is very expensive. The flowers are shaped like ears of wheat. It has many spikes from one root. Sambal, of India origin, is considered the most valuable; it is a rich red ointment with a very fragrant odor.

Squill (*Urginea scilla*)

Folk Names: White squill, red squill, maritime squill

Gender: Hot

Planet: Mars

Element: Fire/Water

Associated Deities: Horus, Ares, Mars, Tiw

Part used: Bulb

Basic Powers: Prosperity, success, psychic visions

Stacte: *See Storax.*

Star Anise (*Illicium verum, I. anisatum*)

Folk Names: Chinese anise

Gender: Hot

Planet: Jupiter

Element: Water

Associated Deities: Jupiter, Zeus, Amun, Odin, Thor

Part Used: Seed

Basic Powers: Clairvoyance

Specific Use: Burn the seeds as an incense to bring clairvoyance or use in making herbal pendulums.

Storax (*Liquidambar orientalis, L. styracifluca*)

Folk Names: Styrax, sweet gum

Gender: Hot

Planet: Sun, sometimes Mercury and Saturn

Element: Fire

Associated Deities: Osiris, Apollo, Horus, Ra, Adonis

Parts Used: Wood, inner bark

Basic Powers: Purification, success

Specific Uses: The balsam obtained from the wood and the inner bark of this tree is used in perfumery and incense. It blends well with oriental (spicy, woody, earthy) scents and serves as a fixative for florals. Note: the storax of the ancients is not this tree, but *Styrax officinale*, a close relative of benzoin.

Sulfur (mineral)

Folk Name: Brimstone

Gender: Cold

Planet: Saturn

Element: Earth

Associated Deities: Isis, Hecate, Nephthys, Demeter, Saturn, Kronos, Ceres, Nut, Cerridwen, Danu

Basic Powers: Protection, exorcism

Specific Uses: I do not recommend using this because of the harmful, choking smoke and foul odor. It can be dangerous to one's health.

Sumbul (*Ferula sumbul*)

Folk Names: Muskroot, jatamansi, ouchi, sumbuluwurzel

Gender: Cold

Planet: Saturn

Element: Earth

Associated Deities: Saturn, Kronos, Nephthys, Isis, Demeter, Ceres, Nut, Danu, Cerridwen, Hecate

Part Used: Root

Basic Powers: Binding, uncrossing, protection

Specific Use: Incense.

Sunflower (*Helianthus annuus*)

Gender: Hot

Planet: Sun

Element: Fire

Associated Deities: Apollo, Bast, Horus, Ra, Adonis

Parts Used: Flower, seeds

Basic Powers: Protection, fertility

Specific Uses: The flowers grown in the garden bring blessings of the sun; they also attract good luck, safety, and protection. The seeds are often eaten by women wanting to conceive; this is done during the waxing moon.

Sweet Bugle (*Lycopus virginicus*)

Folk Names: Bugleweed, water bugle, Virginia water horehound, gipsyweed

Gender: Cold

Planet: Venus

Element: Water

Associated Deities: Venus, Aphrodite, Hathor, Freyja, Kuan Yin, Brigid

Part Used: Herb

Basic Powers: Love, sexual attration

Specific Uses: Incense and sachet bags.

Sweet Flag: *See Calamus.*

Tansy (*Tanacetum vulgare*)

Folk Names: Bitter buttons, hindheal, parsley fern

Gender: Cold

Planet: Venus

Element: Water

Associated Deities: Venus, Aphrodite, Hathor, Freyja, Kuan Yin, Brigid

Part Used: Herb

Basic Powers: Spiritual seeking, reincarnation study

Specific Uses: Among the old uses were as a strewing herb and used as amn embalming ingredient. It has a balsamic odor as well as a lemony fragrance. It can be a narcotic in large doses.

Terebinth (*Pistacia terebinthus*)

Folk Names: Turpentine tree

Gender: Hot

Planet: Jupiter

Element: Fire/Water

Associated Deities: Jupiter, Bel

Part Used: Wood

Basic Powers: Honor, good luck

Specific Uses: This is the Mideastern equivalent of the oak, as it also has very hard wood. It is also sacred to Jupiter and Bel.

Thistle (*Sanchus* spp., *Carbenia benedicta, Cnicus benedictus, Carduus benedictus*)

Folk Names: Holy thistle, blessed thistle

Gender: Hot

Planet: Mars

Element: Fire

Associated Deities: Ares, Mars, Thor, Horus

Part Used: Herb

Basic Power: Protection

Specific Uses: Has a reputation as a heal-all. Throw
into a fire if you fear being struck by lightning
during a storm. Grow in the garden to ward off
thieves. A bowl of thistles in a room strengthens and
energizes those within it.

Thornapple: *See Datura.*

Thyme, Garden (*Thymus vulgaris*); wild thyme (*T. serpyllum*)

Folk Names: Garden thyme, common thyme, mother
of thyme, creeping thyme

Gender: Cold

Planet: Venus

Element: Air

Associated Deities: Venus, Aphrodite, Hathor, Freyja,
Brigid

Part Used: Herb

Basic Powers: Clairvoyance, purification

Specific Uses: Burn as incense to purge and fumigate
magickal rooms. A cleansing bath for springtime
is comprised of thyme and marjoram. A pillow
stuffed with thyme cures nightmares. Wear a spring
of the herb to funerals to protect yourself from the
negativity of the mourners. Used in perfumery and
potpourris. Wild thyme, called mother of thyme,
denotes a pure atmosphere wherever it grows and is
a favorite with fairies.

Tobacco (*Nicotiana tabacum*)

Gender: Hot

Planet: Mars

Element: Fire

Associated Deities: Ares, Mars, Thor, Horus

Parts Used: Leaves. POISONOUS IF EATEN.

Basic Powers: Exorcism, Native American offering to the four directions as blessings

Specific Uses: Used externally only. Used in perfumery and in incense for a masculine, martial effect. Burned on charcoal to remove negativity.

Tonka Bean (*Coumarouna odorata, Dipsteryx odorata*)

Folk Names: Tonqua, tonquin bean, coumara nut

Gender: Cold

Planet: Venus

Element: Water

Associated Deities: Venus, Aphrodite, Hathor, Freyja, Brigid

Part Used: Beans

Basic Power: Love

Specific Uses: Carry the bean in love sachets to attract love. The seeds are used in perfumery, sachets, and other mixtures for their scent and as a fixative. Also carried as love talismans. Said to bring good luck.

Tragacanth (*Astragalus gummifer*)

Folk Names: Gum dragon, Syrian tragacanth

Gender: Cold

Planet: Mercury

Element: Air

Associated Deities: Hermes, Thoth, Anubis, Maat, Odin

Part Used: Gum

Basic Powers: Prediction, intellect, divination, magick

Specific Uses: The gummy exudation contains mucilage and is used to make pastes and to hold powders together. To make scented beads (at one time used for rosaries); mix gum tragacanth with water to make a paste, then add spices and fragrant powdered herbs and flowers, essential oils, and form into beads. Let dry. Pierce with a long needle and string.

Unicorn Root, False (*Chamaelirium luteum*)

Folk Names: Starwort, helonias, veratum luteum

Gender: Cold

Planet: Saturn

Element: Earth

Associated Deities: Isis, Hecate, Nephthys, Demeter

Part Used: Root. POISONOUS

Basic Power: Protection

Specific Uses: Use in incenses to ward off evil. The fresh root is poisonous, so only use it dried or better yet, substitute another herb.

Unicorn Root, True (*Aletris farinosa*)

Folk Names: Stargrass, ague root, devil's bit, colic root

Gender: Cold

Planet: Saturn

Element: Earth

Associated Deities: Isis, Hecate, Nephthys, Demeter

Part Used: Root. POISONOUS

Basic Power: Protection

Specific Uses: *See Unicorn Root, False.*

Uva Ursi (*Arctostaphylos uva-ursi, Arbutus uva ursi*)

Folk Names: Bearberry, kinnikinnick, pinemat, manzanita

Gender: Cold

Planet: Venus

Element: Earth/Air

Associated Deities: Venus, Hathor, Freyja, Brigid

Part Used: Leaves

Basic Powers: Astral travel, spells, conjurations

Specific Uses: Leaves are gathered in September and
October. Do NOT take internally as large doses are
dangerous. Put some leaves in an open bowl in a
room when doing occult work.

Valerian (*Valeriana officinalis*)

Folk Names: Phu, all-heal, amatilla, set well, capon's
tailor, garden heliotrope, vandal root, fragrant
valerian, St. George's herb, setwell, cat's valerian,
English valerian, vandal

Gender: Cold

Planet: Mercury, sometimes Saturn.

Element: Water

Associated Deities: Thoth, Hermes, Anubis, Maat

Parts Used: Herb and root

Basic Powers: Love, harmony

Specific Uses: Use the fresh herbs in love spells; also
to get fighting couples peacefully together. Use in a
purification bath sachet. Some cats find this herb as
enticing as catnip. This can be used in any crossing
spells where graveyard dirt is called for.

Vanilla (*Vanilla aromatic* or *V. planifolia*)

Gender: Hot

Planet: Jupiter

Element: Fire

Associated Deities: Zeus, Osiris, Amun, Thor

Part Used: Bean

Basic Power: Love

Specific Uses: The bean or pod is used in perfumery, sachets, and incenses. In large quantities it is poisonous. Although vanilla is most often used in its oil form, the whole bean is sometimes added to love charms.

Verbena, Lemon (*Aloysia citriodora, Lippis citrodora*)

Folk Names: Verveine citronella, herb Louisa, yerba Louisa

Gender: Hot

Planet: Jupiter

Element: Fire/Water

Associated Deities: Jupiter, Zeus, Amun, Don, the Dagda, Thor

Parts Used: Leaves, flowering tops

Specific Uses: A mild sedative in a tea with an overpowering lemon scent. The leaves grow in sets of three.

Vervain (*Verbena officinalis*)

Folk Names: Juno's tears, herb of grace, pigeon's grass, enchanter's plant, simpler's joy, holy herb, pigeonwood, herb of the cross, verbena, herb of enchantment, vervan, van-van

Gender: Cold

Planet: Venus, sometimes Mercury

Element: Water

Associated Deities: Mars, Venus, Aradia, Cerridwen, Isis, Jupiter, Thor

Part Used: Herb

Basic Powers: Love, purification, protection

Specific Uses: Reputed to be an aphrodisiac, a powerful amulet to ward off psychic attack and evil, and used in many love charms and incenses. Use in magickal cleansing baths, purification incenses, and personal safety amulets. Best gathered at Summer Solstice. Hang by the bed to keep free of nightmares. Burn with equal parts frankincense for a fantastic purification incense. It attracts wealth and the opposite sex. Sacred to many cultures around the world.

Vetiver (*Vetiveria zizanioides*)

Folk Names: Khus khus, vetivert

Gender: Cold

Planet: Venus

Element: Earth/Air

Associated Deities: Hathor, Freyja, Brigid

Part Used: Root

Basic Powers: Love, protection, prosperity

Specific Uses: The root smells like faded violets or sandalwood and is used in perfumery and scent mixtures. It is a fixative for potpourris and blends well with rose.

Vine (*Vitis vinifera*)

Folk name: Grape vine

Gender: Hot

Planet: Sun

Element: Fire

Associated Deities: Bacchus, Dionysus, Osiris, Horus, Ra, Bast, Isis

Parts Used: Fruit and leaves

Basic Powers: Inspiration, physical love

Specific Uses. Called the tree of joy and exhilaration, but also of wrath. Associated with poetic inspiration. The vine's five-pointed leaves make it sacred to the Great Goddess.

Violet (*Viola tricolor* or *V. odorata*)

Folk Names: Blue violet, sweet violet

Gender: Cold

Planet: Venus

Element: Water

Associated Deities: Venus, Aphrodite, Priapus

Part Used: Flowers

Basic Power: Love

Specific Uses: The scent promotes sleep. Also powerful against evil spirits. Extensively used in perfumery, the flowers are used to add blue color to potpourris. Mix with lavender to make a powerful love sachet. It is said that carrying the flowers will bring a change of luck and fortune.

Walnut, Black (*Juglans nigra*)

Folk name: American walnut

Gender: Hot

Planet: Sun

Element: Fire

Associated Deity: Jupiter

Parts Used: Nuts, leaves, bark

Basic Powers: Fertility, healing

Specific Use: Sacred to Jupiter and was considered a food of the gods.

Walnut, English (*Juglans regia*)

Folk Names: Tree of evil, English walnut, Persian walnut, Caucasian walnut

Gender: Hot

Planet: Sun

Element: Fire

Associated Deity: Jupiter

Part Used: Nut

Basic Powers: Fertility, healing

Specific Uses: *J. regia* is a species native to Greece and Asia. Considered a food of the gods. Carry the nut in its shell to promote fertility, strengthen the heart, or ward off rheumatism.

Water Agrimony (*Bidens tripartita*)

Folk Name: Bur marigold

Gender: Cold

Planet: Moon

Element: Water

Associated Deities: Isis Khensu, Kuan Yin, Neith, Diana, Hecate, Selene, Luna, Morrigan

Parts Used: Whole plant

Basic Powers: Purification, visions, dreams, divination

Specific Uses: A lemony scent. It is an astringent and blood purifier. Use in incenses.

Willow, Black American (*Salix nigra*)

Folk Names: Pussy willow, old wives' tongues, cooper's willow, ozier

Gender: Cold

Planet: Moon

Element: Water

Associated Deities: Luna, Selene

Part Used: Bark

Basic Powers: Healing, Divining

Specific Uses: The bark, taken as a tea, is a pain reliever, the original aspirin. A forked branch is used to dowse for water or underground tanks. Plant a willow in the garden to guard your home. Willow groves are believed to give mystic eloquence and poetic skills; the ancients went to these groves to divine by listening to the wind through the tree. The Muses are connected with the willow; the Grove of Persephone, goddess of trances, was a willow grove. A branch of willow with the fuzzy catkins in the house brings good luck and good health. A tea made from the bark was used for intestinal worms and chronic diarrhea. Also used to relieve ovarian pain, and with warm bark compresses, helps with foot bunions and corns.

Willow, White (*Salix alba*, var. species)

Folk Name: European willow

Gender: Cold

Planet: Moon

Parts Used: Bark

Basic Powers: Healing, divining

Specific Use: Same as Black Willow. They grow easily and quickly.

Winter's Bark (*Drimys winteri*)

Folk Names: Winter's cinnamon, wintera aromatic

Gender: Hot

Planet: Sun

Element: Fire

Associated Deities: Horus, Ra, Apollo, Bast, Sekhmet, Lugh, Bel, Adonis

Part Used: Bark

Basic Powers: Success, command, money

Specific Use: May be substituted for cinnamon bark

Winter's Bark, False (*Cinnamodendron corticosum*)

Folk Names: Red canella, mountain cinnamon

Gender: Hot

Planet: Sun

Element: Fire

Associated Deities: Horus, Ra, Apollo, Bast, Sekhmet, Lugh, Bel, Adonis

Part Used: Dried bark

Basic Powers: Success, command, money

Specific Use: May be substituted for cinnamon bark.

Wintergreen (*Gaultheria procumbens*)

Folk Names: Teaberry, boxberry, mountain tea, checkerberry, aromatic wintergreen, partridge berry, Deerberry

Gender: Cold

Planet: Moon

Element: Water

Associated Deities: Isis, Khensu,. Neith, Hecate, Morrighan

Part Used: Leaves

Basic Powers: Visions, magick

Specific Uses: Contains an aspirin derivative. Use in charm bags and incense.

Witch Hazel (*Hamamelis virginiana*)

Folk Names: Spotted alder, tobacco wood, winterbloom

Gender: Cold

Planet: Moon

Element: Water

Associated Deities: Isis, Diana, Morrighan, Selene

Parts Used: Nuts, leaves, bark, twigs

Basic Powers: Divination, healing

Specific Uses: Forked divining rods are used for finding water. The leaves, bark, and young twigs can be used as a tonic, but they are also astringent, cleansing, styptic, and a slight sedative.

Woodruff (*Asperula odorata*)

Folk Names: Sweet woodruff, master of the woods, woodrove, wuderove, woodruffe, herb walter

Gender: Hot

Planet: Mars

Element: Fire

Associated Deities: Ares, Mars, Thor, Horus

Part Used: Herb

Basic Power: Purification

Specific Uses: Wonderfully fragrant; acquires its scent only as it dries. Used in perfumery and bath herb mixtures. Use it in incense in spring to clear away the closeness and drab atmosphere of the winter.

Carry it to be victorious and turn over a new leaf or your outlook on life.

Wormwood (*Artemisia absinthium*)

Folk Names: Old woman, absinthe, crown for a king

Gender: Hot

Planet: Mars, sometimes the moon

Element: Air

Associated Deities: Diana, Isis, Artemis

Part Used: Herb

Basic Powers: Clairvoyance, protection

Specific Uses: A very magickal herb sacred to the Moon. Use in charms, incense, scrying, divination, prophecy, and astral projections. Works well in incenses containing mugwort and for exorcism blends.

Yarrow (*Achillea millefolium*)

Folk Names: Seven year's love, sangrinary, old man's mustard, military herb, old man's pepper, soldier's woundwort, knight's milfoil, nosebleed, thousand seal, hundred-leaved grass, millefolium, milfoil, arrow root, ladies' mantle, knyghtan, wound wort stanch weed, field hops, tansy, gearwe, noble yarrow, devil's bit, Achillea, snake's grass, Stanch grass

Gender: Cold

Planet: Venus

Element: Water

Associated Deities: Venus, Aphrodite, Hathor, Freyja

Part Used: Flowers

Basic Powers: Love, clairvoyance, exorcism

Specific Uses: Used in divination spells and to consult the I Ching. Sleep with yarrow under one's pillow for dreams of a future spouse. Has the power to keep a couple together happily for seven years. Worn as an amulet, it wards off negativity. Sometimes added to exorcism incenses. In ancient China, it was considered a sacred plant with spiritual qualities.

Yellow Dock (*Rumex crispus*)

Folk Names: Curled dock, narrow dock, sour dock

Gender: Hot

Planet: Jupiter

Element: Fire/Water

Associated Deities: Jupiter, Zeus, Amun, Don, the Dagda, Thor

Part Used: Root

Basic Powers: Prosperity, success, good luck

Specific Use: The powder of this herb stains things with a powerful yellow color. To gain money and/

or prosperity, sprinkle a little inside your mailbox or across the doorway into your place of business.

Yerba Buena (*Satureja douglasii*)

Gender: Cold

Planet: Saturn

Element: Earth

Associated Deities: Saturn, Kronos, Nephthys, Isis, Demeter, Ceres, Nut, Cerridwen, Danu, Hecate

Part Used: Leaves

Basic Powers: Hexing, binding, protection

Specific Use: Add to incenses.

Yerba Maté (*Ilex paraguariensis*)

Folk Names: Paraguay herb, mate, Jesuit's tea, Brazil tea

Gender: Cold

Planet: Saturn

Element Earth

Associated Deities: Saturn, Kronos, Nephthys, Isis, Demeter, Ceres, Nut, Cerridwen, Danu, Hecate

Part Used: Leaves

Basic Powers: Cursing, binding, protection

Specific Uses: Use to stuff poppets. If burned in incense, has a very unpleasant odor.

Yerba Santa (*Eriodictyon glutinosum, E. californicum*)

Folk Names: Mountain balm, consumptive's weed, gum bush, beer's weed, tarweed

Gender: Hot

Planet: Jupiter

Element: Fire/Water

Associated Deities: Jupiter, Zeus, Amun, Dôn, the Dagda, Thor

Part Used: Leaves

Basic Powers: Riches, honor, health

Specific Uses: Southwest Native American peoples smoked, chewed, and brewed it into a tea. The tea is good and has a pleasingly sweet aftertaste.

Yew (*Taurus baccata*)

Folk Names: Chinwood, English yew, European yew

Gender: Cold

Planet: Saturn

Element: Earth

Associated Deities: Hecate, Saturn, Cerridwen, Danu

Part Used: Wood. Do not burn or ingest—POISONOUS.

Basic Powers: Knowledge, reincarnation.

Specific Uses: Symbolizes death and endings, and rules the eve of Winter Solstice. Bows and dagger handles were made of it, as its wood is very hard.

Yohimbe (*Corynanthe yohimbe*), DANGEROUS

Folk Names: Johimbe, yohimbehe

Gender: Cold

Planet: Venus

Element: Earth/Air

Associated Deities: Venus, Aphrodite, Hathor, Freyja, Kuan Yin, Brigid

Part Used: Bark

Basic Powers: Psychic visions, love, sexual attraction

Specific Uses: Considered an aphrodisiac, but large doses cause hallucinations. Not recommended.

If you want to grow some of your own herbs, container planting works well with some of the plants, such as basil, calendula, cayenne, chamomile, echinacea, garlic, ginger, lavender, lemon balm, peppermint, plantain, rosemary, sage, spearmint, thyme, turmeric, yarrow, and red clover.

Eight

Herbal Combinations for Spells

Although this book generally goes beyond the usual physical herbal healing, I want to present several physical formulae that may be of help. Then I will move on to the mental, emotional, and spiritual uses of herbs.

Menstrual Difficulties Tea

1 teaspoon chopped cinnamon bark

1 teaspoon chopped ginger or finely grated ginger root

Honey to sweeten

Pour one cup of boiling water over the herbs. Cover and steep for thirty to forty minutes. Strain and sweeten with honey if desired. A very old formula for the same complaint was sassafras tea, made in a similar manner.

Cold and Flu Tea

Fill a half-pint jar with local honey. Local honey is better because it helps to aid against local allergies. Add half a stick of cinnamon and the juice of a lemon slice (or the slice itself). Let this sit in a warm place for five or six days to meld the mixture. Then keep the jar in the refrigerator. To use, put a teaspoon of the mix in a cup of very hot water to soothe the throat and sinuses.

Four Thieves Vinegar

This is an ancient antiseptic formula that was said to protect thieves from the Black Plague when they were robbing the victims. It makes a good disinfectant. However, you also can take one to two tablespoons every three to four hours to ward off an illness, such as a cold. It also works for spraying down countertops and door knobs as a disinfectant.

4 cloves of garlic, finely chopped

½ cup lavender flowers

¼ cup rosemary leaves

½ cup sage leaves, coarsely chopped

Apple cider vinegar

Put the garlic and herbs into a wide mouth jar and pour in enough warmed vinegar to cover them. Let sit in a warm place for three to four weeks. Strain out the herbs. Pour the vinegar into a clean glass jar with a tight-fitting lid. Let it stand in a cool, dark place; it will keep for a year.

Cider of Fire

This is a really effective mixture for keeping cold and flu away. It can also be used as a salad dressing.

1 medium onion, chopped

4 to 5 cloves of garlic, coarsely chopped

3 to 4 tablespoons freshly grated ginger root

3 to 4 tablespoons grated horseradish (you can use the bottled kind)

Apple cider vinegar

Honey

A pinch of cayenne pepper

Combine the onion, garlic, ginger, and horseradish in a wide mouth quart jar. Pour over these enough warmed vinegar to cover and sit in a warm place for three to four weeks. Strain out the herbs. Add honey and cayenne to taste. Take one to two tablespoons at the first sign of a cold, and repeat every three to four hours until the symptoms are gone.

Calendula Oil Salve

Pack a pint jar with as many calendula (pot marigold) blossoms as possible. Cover with warm almond or light olive oil. Let sit in a warm place for three to four weeks. Strain out the flowers using a piece of cheesecloth to get as much out as possible. If you want a stronger oil, replace with more blossoms and let set again. One cup of this will be used in the next formula. Bottle the rest of the calendula oil in a dark bottle, and store in a cool, dark place. This salve can be used on cuts, wounds, rashes, and diaper rash. Use in small amounts and massage in gently.

1 cup calendula oil

¼ cup grated or granular beeswax

4 to 6 drops essential lavender oil

1 pinch of turmeric powder, if you want a deeper
  yellow color

Warm the oil over a very low heat and stir in the beeswax; add the lavender oil. If you want a softer salve, add more oil. If you want a firmer salve, add a little more beeswax. Stir in the turmeric if you want a golden color. Pour into small jars or tins with lids; label. If stored in a cool, dark place, it will keep for up to a year. If you pierce a vitamin E capsule and add to the leftover oil, or add one drop of liquid benzoin, the oil will keep for a year if capped and kept in the refrigerator. Benzoin is a fixative, as is vitamin E.

Calming Massage Oil

1½ ounces dried lavender buds

4 ounces almond oil

5 to 10 drops essential lavender oil

Put the buds into a clean glass jar, and pour the oil over them. Set the jar in a warm, sunny place for two to three weeks with the lid on. Strain out the buds. Put the essential lavender oil into the other oil drop by drop until you reach the scent you want. To use this for massage, pour a few drops into one hand, rub hands together, and massage the body. It is a good idea to always massage toward the heart. The legs and arms are massaged from the fingers/toes upward, the shoulders and neck downwards.

A few drops of this formula can also be used for a relaxing herbal bath. Just take care not to fall while getting in or out, as the oil will make the tub slippery.

Achy Joints Rub

Be very careful with this formula—don't touch any delicate body parts, the eyes, or face. Wash your hands thoroughly after using it.

½ cup light olive or almond oil

1 to 2 teaspoons cayenne pepper

A few drops of essential wintergreen oil

Beeswax, grated or granular

Combine the first three ingredients, and warm over low heat. Since it is impossible to strain out the cayenne, let it settle to the bottom. Pour the oil, excluding the cayenne at the bottom, into a pan. Add grated or granular beeswax to the oil in the pan until it is thick enough to make a salve. Pour into small jars or tins; label. Rub a small amount on painful joints to soothe and relieve. Always carefully wash your hands afterward.

Fever Tea

If treating a child ages three to six, give them ¼ cup of tea every two hours. If under age three, give one teaspoon per year of age. For a persistent or high fever, see a doctor. An adult can take ½ to one cup of this tea every two hours.

    One part catnip leaf

    1 part elderberry flowers

    1 part spearmint leaf

    Honey to sweeten

Put the three herbs into a glass quart jar. Pour boiling hot water over them. Cap and let steep for 30 to 45 minutes. Strain out the herbs. Pour out and heat the amount needed, adding honey to taste at this time. Recap the remaining liquid.

Clover Tea

Purple or red clover is not as popular with bees as white clover. However, an infusion made from red clover blossoms can be helpful for bronchial problems. It is also an old formula for cancer, although I doubt its efficacy in that department.

   1 ounce of red clover blossoms

   1 pint boiling water

Let steep for 30 to 45 minutes. Have the patient drink a cupful of this hot tea every hour.

Pregnancy Tea

Tea from raspberry leaves has been used for centuries by pregnant women to help with morning sickness and to help ease the troubles of childbirth. The dried leaves are crumbled and put into a teaball or strainer; fill the cup with hot water and let steep for at least five minutes. Sweeten with honey if desired. It can be taken several times a day.

Chest Congestion Cough Syrup

Slice one cut raw onion and put into a small stainless steel or glass cooking pan with a lid. Add enough raw honey to cover the onion (about half a cup) and simmer, slowing until the onion bits are almost dissolved; leave the lid on during this cooking; the process takes about 20 minutes. Strain and store the syrup in the refrigerator. Can be taken up to once every half hour in one tablespoon doses for adults.

Medicinal Basil Pesto

½ to 1 cup olive oil

1 to 3 garlic cloves

½ cup fresh basil leaves

½ cup fresh dandelion leaves

1 cup fresh cilantro leaves and stems

½ to 1 cup walnuts

¼ cup grated hard Parmesan cheese

Combine the oil, garlic, and fresh greens in a blender or food processor until smooth. Add nuts and cheese, and pulse again until the desired consistency. Freeze in an ice cube tray for proportion size. Then empty frozen cubes into a freezer bag. Use on crackers, pasta, or in soup.

Thyme Cough/Cold/Chest Syrup

2 to 4 ounces thyme leaves

1 quart water

1 cup honey

Combine thyme and water over very low heat, simmering with the lid ajar. When liquid is reduced to 2 cups, strain the strong tea and add the honey, stirring until melted. Store in a glass jar in the refrigerator for up to four weeks. Use ½ to 1 teaspoon every couple of hours until the cough stops.

Turmeric Arthritis/Bursitis/Immune System

¼ cup turmeric root powder

almond oil

almond milk

honey to sweeten

To make the base of this mixture, combine the turmeric power with ½ cup water in a pan. Boil, then simmer until a thick paste is formed. Cool and scoop this paste into a glass jar and store in refrigerator. To make one serving, combine ½ to 1 teaspoon of the paste, 1 teaspoon of almond oil, and 1 cup of almond milk in a blender. Add honey to sweeten. Blend to make a frothy drink. Cinnamon and ginger may also be added.

Garlic Ear Oil

1 to 2 cloves of garlic, peeled and sliced

2 tablespoons of olive oil

Combine garlic and oil in the top of a double boiler. Warm over very low heat for 10 to 15 minutes, or until the oil smells like garlic. Carefully strain all garlic through a sieve with cheesecloth. Pour the oil into small glass dropper bottles and store in the refrigerator for several months. To use for ear infections connected to colds and respiratory problems, gently warm the bottle in a pan of hot water to barely warm. Put several drops in both ears and gently massage the ears. Repeat every 30 minutes until the pain stops. Mullein flowers may be used in place of the garlic.

Motion Sickness Balls

2 tablespoons ginger root powder

1 to 2 tablespoons unsweetened cocoa powder

1 tablespoon cinnamon powder

honey to sweeten

Combine the ginger, cocoa, and cinnamon in a bowl. Mix in enough honey until mixture is like bread dough. Add ½ teaspoon water and knead a few minutes. If necessary, add more ginger or cocoa powder. Roll into pea-sized balls. Dry at room temperature. Keep in a cold, dark place like the refrigerator. Take 2 to 3 balls an hour before traveling, then as needed.

Sage Sore Throat Gargle

1 tablespoon dried sage leaves

1 to 2 tablespoon salt

1 teaspoon goldenseal root powder

a few grains of cayenne

½ cup apple cider vinegar

Pour ½ cup boiling water over the dried sage. Cover and let steep 45 minutes. Stir in salt, goldenseal, and cayenne, then the apple cider vinegar. Gargle a teaspoon of this every 30 minutes to one hour. Don't swallow—it tastes bad!

Migraine Tincture

1 tablespoon California leaf and flower

1 tablespoon lavender buds

1 tablespoon feverfew leaves

80 proof alcohol (or apple cider vinegar)

Put finely chopped herbs in a clean dry glass jar with a lid. Pour enough cider vinegar to cover the herbs by two inches. Put in a warm sunny place for 4 to 6 weeks; shake daily. Strain the herbs into a clean jar; cap and label. This should keep up to a year. For frequent headaches, take ½ teaspoon two times a day for up to three months. Discontinue for 3 to 4 weeks. Women should not take when pregnant and should discontinue during menstruation as it can stimulate bleeding.

Gypsy Cold Remedy

½ cup elder flowers

½ cup peppermint leaf

½ cup yarrow flowers and leaf

Put chopped herbs in a clean glass jar with a lid. Pour boiling water over the herbs, filling the jar. Let steep for 45 minutes to make a very strong tea. Strain out the herbs. Warm and sip throughout the day.

Eye Packs

2 chamomile tea bags

water for tea

These help with eye strain, dark circles, and puffiness. Place two chamomile teabags in hot water and let sit a couple of minutes. Remove and let the bags cool until tolerable to the skin. Place a tea bag on each eye. Drink the tea while relaxing with tea bags in place for 15 to 20 minutes.

Gypsy Fever-Reducing Tea

1 cup elder flowers

1 cup yarrow flowers and leaf

1 cup peppermint leaf

Chop herbs and put in a clean glass jar with a lid. Cover with boiling water and steep for 45 minutes. Strain out herbs. Drink ½ cup every 30 minutes to bring on a good sweat and continue until fever lessens.

Kidney Stone Relief Tincture

½ teaspoon California poppy flower tincture

⅓ teaspoon Jamaican dogwood bark tincture

¼ teaspoon juniper berry tincture

½ teaspoon marshmallow root tincture

⅛ teaspoon dandelion root tincture

⅛ teaspoon turmeric root tincture

Add tinctures to one ounce water. Drink one ounce every 20 minutes until pain subsides.

Live Forever Salve

This is good for poison oak, poison ivy, or poison sumac.

1 pound of lard

1 cup of Live Forever leaf (*Sedum purpuream*) leaves, washed and dried

Over medium heat in a skillet, cook the herbs until the leaves are brown and the lard turns green. Strain and put into a clean jar with a lid. Apply as necessary.

Horehound Lozenges

The green herb is mixed with honey as a good remedy for all chest complaints. It can also be used as candied lozenges for hoarseness, cough, and catarrh. To make lozenges:

⅓ cup of dried leaves

4 cups brown sugar

1 teaspoon cream of tartar

1 teaspoon butter

Steep leaves in two cups of boiling water for an hour and strain. To this add two cups of liquid, add the brown sugar and cream of tartar. Heat to a temperature of 220° Fahrenheit. Add one teaspoon butter (do not stir) and pour into buttered pans. Mark into squares and cool. Large doses of horehound will also expel worms.

Tea Bags and Raisins

Raisins are a good remedy for recurring boils and carbuncles. They are also a good and gentle source of iron.

Tea bags are also a handy remedy for boils and pockets of infection. However, the tea bags must be the caffeinated type; the non-caffeinated kind will not work. My sister, a retired nurse, often used this remedy (with unofficial) doctor's approval in the nursing homes where she worked.

Carrot Poultice

Shred and heat in enough water to cover the carrots. Strain and spread on a clean cloth. Check that the mixture is not too hot on the skin. Place over the infected body part. Remove when cool to the touch. Carrots are a very strong antiseptic.

Potato Poultice

Cool a baked potato so it doesn't burn the skin. Cut it in half and tie the potato over a boil or infected spot to bring the infection to a head.

Lemon Balm Tea

This is best when the lemon balm is fresh with its delightful lemon fragrance. Drink as a tea to induce a mild perspiration and ease the pain of a fever. It also helps revive a tired brain.

Itchy Scalp

The orange-scented leaves of bergamot are made into a tea that can be used as a diuretic. Mixed with apple cider vinegar it is also used for dandruff or an itchy scalp.

Panic Attacks

1 part California poppy flowers and/or seeds

1 part chamomile

½ part marshmallow root

Prepare as an infusion or tea. This is a very gentle formula that can be drunk as much and as often as needed. To make a good medicinal tea, pour boiling water over the herbs, cover, and steep for five minutes. Strain and drink, using a little honey to sweeten if desired.

Burns

My grandmother would immediately plunge the burned area in cold running water to keep the heat from going farther into the skin. Third-degree burns and staph infections require a doctor's care. Dry the area gently, then apply aloe vera gel to the burned area and let it dry there. Aloe vera is a disinfecting, cooling, and healing herb. I keep both a plant and a bottle of the aloe vera gel.

St. John's wort salve is also good for healing burns, even sunburn. It can also be used for cuts, rashes, and wounds.

To make a salve, begin by making an herb-infused oil. Choose cold-pressed almond oil, light olive oil, or jojoba oil. Using a double-boiler pan with a lid, combine the herb and oil in the top pot. Bring to a low simmer and heat for 30 to 60 minutes. Check frequently to be certain the oil isn't overheating. The lower the heat, the longer the infusion, and the better the oil. Strain through cheesecloth or muslin. Wring out the cloth thoroughly to get every drop.

To make a salve, use this oil. To each cup of herbal oil, add ¼ cup of beeswax. Heat until the beeswax is melted. Put one tablespoon of oil into the freezer for a minute to check if it is too soft or hard. If too soft, add more wax. If too hard, add more oil. Remove from heat and pour into small glass jars or tins.

To make St. John's wort salve, make an herbal oil using one part calendula flowers, one part comfrey leaf, and one part St. John's wort leaf and flower. Add beeswax to the oil and pour into jars.

Nerve Tonic

To make an herbal tea or infusion, you need a quart jar with a tight-fitting lid, boiling water and herbs. Put the herbs in the jar; fill the jar with boiling water and cap. Use twice as much fresh herbs as dried. Strain out herbs. Store in the refrigerator for three to four days. Left out, it will sour.

3 parts lemon balm

1 part chamomile

½ part chrysanthemum flowers

½ part rose petals

¼ part lavender flowers

Honey to sweeten, if desired

Drink daily for two to three months. Drink one cup three or four times a day.

Cough and Sore Throat Syrup

To make a syrup, you can substitute maple syrup or vegetable glycerin, although I prefer using honey. The family's recipe for this syrup with honey always tasted better than when made with other liquids. Use two ounces of herb mixture to one quart water. Over low heat, simmer down to one pint. Strain the herbs from the liquid, and put the liquid back into the pan. To each pint of liquid, add one cup honey. You can add more if you prefer it sweeter. Warm together only enough to blend well. When this is done, you can add two drops of peppermint or a small amount to help preserve the syrup and to relax a cough. Remove from the heat, bottle, and label. Syrups will last weeks, even months, if refrigerated.

4 parts fennel seed

2 parts licorice root

2 parts slippery elm bark

2 parts valerian

2 parts wild cherry bark

1 part cinnamon bark

½ part ginger root

⅛ part orange peel

Make into a syrup. Take 1 to 2 teaspoons every hour or two throughout the day or when having a bout of coughing.

Ginger Syrup/Jam

Good for a cold, stomach cramps, motion sickness, coughs, or menstrual discomfort.

Peel a large clump of fresh ginger root. Grate it and put in a pan. Add just enough honey to barely cover the ginger. Simmer over low heat for 10 to 15 minutes, until the ginger root is soft and mushy. Honey will taste strongly of ginger. Do not strain. The ginger will be soft and add texture. Pour into a glass jar and refrigerate. Can be eaten as a jam.

Use 1 tablespoon as needed, or add 2 to 3 tablespoons to a cup of hot water for hot ginger tea.

Anticold Salad

Combine finely cut tomatoes, red onions, mashed garlic buds, vegetable oil, and lemon juice. Eat at least once a day when a cold starts.

Anti-Flu/Cold Remedy

Use gloves when handling cayenne pepper and avoid touching your eyes, face, or private parts. Cayenne is almost impossible to remove from the skin once you touch yourself.

1½ teaspoons salt

2 teaspoons cayenne pepper

1 cup boiling water

1 cup apple cider vinegar

Grind the salt and cayenne together to make a paste. Add the boiling water; steep and cool. Add the vinegar to the water. Most adults can take a teaspoon to a tablespoon every half to one hour.

Achy Joints Rub

½ cup light olive oil

1 tablespoon cayenne powder

⅛ cup beeswax

Few drops of wintergreen essential oil

Mix the oil and cayenne in top pan of a double boiler; heat to a very low simmer with just a few bubbles rising. Do not overheat. Simmer gently for 30 to 60 minutes. Mix in the beeswax and essential oil. Pour into small jars.

Rub a small amount over achy joints for pain. Do not cover the joint as the held-in heat will make you feel like your skin is on fire! In fact, instead of using your bare skin to apply, use a rubber glove or piece of fabric. Do not put near anyone's eyes, face, or private parts.

Magickal Combinations

The success of a spell or wish is influenced by many things, starting with the deep intent you have clearly in mind. The mind, the body, the emotions, and the spiritual path all must work together to gain your goal. If any of these are out of balance, they are all affected. To help strengthen the spells I'm giving you additional information on stones and colors that will help stir the mental, emotional, and spiritual sides of you to heal and work the spell more effectively.

Stones by Color

Black: binding; defense by repelling dark magick; transforming negative spells and thoughtforms into positive energy; general defense; release from feeling bound

Blue: Harmony; understanding; journeys or moves; healing

Brown: Contacting Earth elementals; success; amplifies all Earth magick and psychic abilities; common sense

Green: Marriage; relationships; balance; practical creativity particularly with the hands; fertility; growth; money

Indigo: Discovering past lives; understanding karmic problems; balancing out karma; stopping undesirable habits or experiences

Orange: Change your luck; power, control of a situation

Pink: Healing; true love; friendship

Purple: Breaking bad luck; protection; psychic and spiritual growth; success in long range plans

Red: Courage to face a conflict or test; energy; taking action

White: Spiritual guidance; being directed into the right paths; calmness; becoming centered; seeing past all illusions

Yellow: Power of the mind; creativity of a mental nature; sudden changes

Clear quartz crystal: Psychic work; helps with divinations; amplifies the power raised during all spellwork

Lodestone or magnetite: Drawing power; ability to attract what you desire

Moonstone: Gaining occult power; soothing the emotions; rising above problems; Moon deities

Pyrite or fool's gold: Money; prosperity; total success; sun deities

There are four important inner biomagnetic sheaths, or auras, around the human body. Each is linked with vital body chakras or power centers. To realign these sheaths and power centers, place certain stones on the body, or wear jewelry with power stones in it.

Grounding energy from the crown of the head to the feet: Smoky
   quartz

Opening and cleansing all: Amber, malachite

Cleansing and protecting all: Garnet, tourmaline

Aligning in general: Yellow kunzite, kyanite

It is also possible to make gem elixirs or essence. To make
an elixir, place a cleansed stone into a glass bowl with spring
water or filtered water. If the stone is friable or the dust considered toxic, put the stone into a small glass jar and then
into the glass bowl. Set in the sunlight for twelve hours.
Remove the stone and pour the elixir into a clean glass bottle with an airtight lid. To keep for more than a week, add 50
percent brandy or vodka as a preservative. Store in a cool,
dark place. Be sure to label.

To make a dosage bottle, add seven drops of the mother
elixir to a glass dropper bottle. Fill with ⅓ brandy to ⅔
water if taking by mouth or putting on the skin. If using in
the eyes, omit the alcohol. Take seven drops three times a
day. Following is a list of stones and what their elixirs do.

Agate, Blue Lace: Eye infections

Agate, Moss: Fungal infections

Amazonite: Balances the metabolism

Amber: Antibiotic, deals with throat problems

Beryl, Golden: Gargle for sore throats

Bloodstone: Release constipation and emotional stagnation

Charoite: Excellent cleanser for the body

Fluorite: Breaks up blockages; anti-viral

Hematite: Strengthens boundaries in the sheaths

Herkimer Diamond: Aids psychic vision and dream recall

Jadeite: Eye conditions; brings peace

Jasper, Green: Restores biorhythms

Kunzite: Opens the heart

Malachite (tumbled only): Harmonizes physical, mental, emotional, and spiritual

Tourmaline, Black: Releases toxic energy from the emotions, mind, and body

Stones by Magickal Powers

Agate: Regains balance in life; settles conflicts; courage, good luck

Amazonite: Self-confidence

Amber: Draws off negative energy

Amethyst: Cleans the aura's shields and protects them; draws in divine energy; helps to gain spiritual blessings; removes tensions and stress

Apache Tear: Keeps the aura from absorbing negative energy

Aventurine: Change of luck

Bloodstone: Spiritual cleanser; binds troublesome people

Carnelian: Repelling ill-wishing

Citrine: Cleans and aligns the auras; prosperity

Fluorite: Psychic shield

Fossils: Surviving problems

Garnet: Relieves depression; courage

Hematite: Court cases, lawyers; overcoming obstacles; will power

Iolite: Handling unwanted situations

Jade: Shields against negative vibrations

Jade, Black: Guards against negatives

Kunzite: A very spiritual stone that dispels negatives and removes obstacles

Labradorite: Prevents energy leaks

Lapis Lazuli: Spiritual growth

Magnitite: Alleviates negative emotions; attracts love, commitment, and loyalty

Malachite: Lifts spirits when totally discouraged

Moonstone: Uncovers secrets and deceptions; helps in gaining psychic abilities; reveals secret enemies

Obsidian: Stops psychic attacks

Peridot: Dissolves jealousy

Pyrite: Prosperity

Quartz, Clear: Cleans, protects, energizes; guardian angels; inner guidance; inspiration; solving problems

Quartz, Rose: Finding true love

Quartz, Smoky: Grounds energy and dissolves negative patterns

Sard: Handling family problems

Selenite: Pinpoints issues and lessons that need to be worked on and leads to ways to solve them

Tiger's Eye: Resolves dilemmas and internal conflicts

Tourmaline: Psychic shield; helps in dealing with fear; release guilt

Tourmaline, Green: Heals holes in the aura

The stones do not have to be faceted or expensive. They do not even have to be tumbled smooth, large, or of the best quality. As you can see in the lists, some stones are multi-functional so you don't even need a different one for each spell unless you are trying to do more than one spell at a time (which isn't advised). Handle several stones of a kind to see which feels right to you. You can keep them in a plastic bag with a label until you can differentiate between the types of stones. Most of the stones can, and should be rinsed in water to cleanse them of all vibrations except yours. One exception is calcite, which is too soft to endure water. You can cleanse calcite by surrounding it with quartz crystals for twenty-four hours.

When your spell is completed, and you empty the used herbs on the ground, pick up and cleanse the used stones again. Stones shouldn't be wasted; they are not an infinite resource.

Stones make charm bags and poppets more powerful, which is why I've listed them. You can go only by the color of the stones if you wish, but more energy is drawn to your project if certain stones are used.

The following list for the planets will help you decide on the weekday, if you want to further fine-tune your project and energy. This list will also work if you desire to use a certain hour of the day.

Planetary Notes

Sun—Sunday

Personal power, health, success, self-confidence,
vitality, courage, authority, dignity, fame,
self-knowledge

Color: Orange or gold

Stones: Yellow jasper, topaz

Herbs: Angelica, bay, calendula, frankincense, juniper,
rosemary, St. John's Wort, sunflower

Moon—Monday

Dreamwork, the inner self, psychic knowledge, dream
working, childbirth, fertility, past life recall, imagination,
subconscious mind

Color: Violet, silver

Stones: Moonstone, pearl, abalone, selenite

Herbs: Jasmine, almond, iris, lily, lotus, moonwort,
mugwort, violet, white sandalwood

Mars—Tuesday

Courage, motivation, victory, aggression, achievement,
energy, action, assertiveness, strength

Color: Scarlet, red

Stones: Garnet, ruby, carnelian, bloodstone

Herbs: Honeysuckle, basil, cactus, cayenne, dragon's blood resin, galangal, garlic, ginger, hawthorn, nettle, red sandalwood, rue

Mercury—Wednesday

Communication, knowledge, business, divination, business success, learning

Color: Yellow

Stones: Quartz, opal, Herkimer diamond, yellow calcite, yellow jasper

Herbs: Bergamot, caraway, cinnamon, dill, gum Arabic, gum mastic, horehound, lavender, marjoram, mullein, peppermint, star anise, savory, thyme

Jupiter—Thursday

Prosperity, honor, expansion, career, ambition, luck, material success, spiritual growth, humor

Color: royal blue, purple

Stones: Sapphire, turquoise, blue topaz, lapis lazuli

Herbs: Borage, carnation, cedar, cinquefoil, dandelion, fir, hyssop, magnolia, maple, meadowsweet, oak moss, pine, popular, sage, sassafras

Venus—Friday

Love, the arts, friendships, artistry, attraction, music, pleasure, sensual delight, beauty, balance, compassion.

Color: Green

Stones: Emerald, malachite, apatite, green fluorite

Herbs: Catnip, coltsfoot, feverfew, lemon verbena,
lilac, myrtle, passion flower, peach, periwinkle,
raspberry, rose, tonka bean, vanilla, vervain, violet

Saturn-Saturday

Grounding, protection, stability, karmic lessons.

Color: Indigo, black

Stones: Jet, onyx, hematite, smoky quartz

Herbs: Balm of Gilead, boneset, comfrey, cypress, dill,
garlic, hawthorn, hyssop, patchouli, rosemary, St.
John's Wort, valerian, vetiver

I've given you a wide variety of herbs and stones to use in your spells or prayers. Choose the ones that you feel good about using and/or are within your budget. The power of your intent will be what makes them all work together to fulfill your wish.

You can see in illustrations that poppets and charm bags don't have to be very large. In fact, small is often better. You can pin a small charm bag to the inside of your bra or easily carry it in your pocket. A poppet can just as easily fit into a drawer. That way no one sees it and thinks you are up to some negative mischief. Fill most of the poppet or charm bag with cotton balls or quilt batting. You will be putting a lot of your intent energy into the spoonful of herbs you will add.

The poppet is primarily used for healing on yourself or others. You can draw on facial features. Poppets are stuffed with appropriate herbs and a stone (or stones) placed inside where the illness is. The poppet will require two cut pieces of muslin or fabric, so just sew up the sides first and leave a small opening to stuff in the herbs and stones. Then finish sewing the poppet shut.

The same procedure is used with a charm bag. Sew three sides shut, stuff in the herbs and stones, then sew the packet closed. You can also use fabric glue instead of sewing. The charm bag needs only one piece of fabric cut, as it will be bent in half, the two sides sewed or glued together, and then the top closed after the herbs are inside.

Following are some examples for both poppet and charm bags. You can choose different herbs and stones if you wish. You also can change the chant or make up your own. The most important part is to be clear in your intent and concentrate on it very hard while holding the finished poppet or charm bag.

Changing Your Luck Charm Bag

Herbs: Basil, frankincense, equal amounts of each. Grind the basil fine, but don't grind the frankincense. Frankincense has a tendency to ball into a sticky mess, so try to purchase it in powder form or very small granules. Create a charm that says "money," "good luck," or something similar. Fill the charm bag and seal it, either by sewing or gluing. Hold the bag between your hands and concentrate very hard on your intent of changing your luck.

Chant: "Bad luck now leaves me. I shed no tears over the parting. Open my life to accept good luck."

Influence Someone to Repay a Debt Sachet

Herbs: One part each: clove, ginger, jasmine, allspice

Add a small piece of hematite and tiger's eye. Seal the bag. Hold the bag between your hands and concentrate on the person repaying the debt.

Chant: "What was given in trust shall be freely returned. What was mine shall be mine again."

Healing Poppet

Herbs: One part each jasmine and myrrh. Two drops gardenia oil.

Stuff the herbs into a cotton-filled poppet along with a small piece of fluorite or beryl. Say: "I name you (name of sick person)." Concentrate of the person being healed and whole again.

Chant: "I call in the Light of healing to fill the body, mind, and spirit of (name). The Light cannot be denied its healing powers. No one and nothing can stop it from its cleansing path. I draw down the Healing Light! I draw down the Light!"

Put the poppet in a safe place, out of sight. Hold the poppet and repeat the chant for seven nights. When the healing comes, empty the herbs onto the ground. Retrieve and wash the stone carefully so it can be used again. The poppet can then be disposed in whatever manner you wish.

Herbal Teas

Dried herbs, especially for teas, should be kept in airtight containers. Most herbs require using one teaspoon dried herbs or two tablespoons fresh herbs to one cup of water. When drinking the tea for pleasure, not medicine, adjust the herbs to suit your taste.

Make an infusion by pouring boiling water over the herbs and allow them to steep for ten to thirty minutes. Keep the tea container tightly closed or covered.

A decoction is the preferred method for brewing most roots, barks, and hard nuts or seeds. Make by simmering the herbs in boiling water for fifteen to thirty minutes. Keep the pot tightly covered.

Spicy Flavors

Nutmeg: Don't use too much; spicy flavor

Cloves: Hot, spicy, aromatic; add only a few buds

Cinnamon: Warming, fragrant, pleasant

Ginger: Energizing, warming; avoid too much or the tea will taste hot

Lemon Flavors

Lemon peel: Bitter if brewed too long

Lemon balm: Good when fresh; rather bland when dried

Lemongrass: Fragrant, delicious and high in vitamin A

Orange peel: Very tangy and fragrant but bitter if brewed too long

Mint Flavors

Spearmint: Classic mint, blends flavors well

Peppermint: Strong, calming flavor

Wintergreen: Woodsy mint

Tart Flavors

Rose hips: Refreshingly tart

Hibiscus: Very tart and rich in vitamin C

Sweet Flavors

Licorice: Sweet flavored

Anise seed: Licorice flavored

Fennel: Sweet licorice flavored

Vanilla bean: Chop for a rich vanilla flavor

Flowers

Chamomile: Fragrant and bittersweet; bitter if brewed too long

Roses: Mildly relaxing, delicious flavor

Lavender: violet color and pungent flavor

Woodsy Flavor

Star anise: Wonderful with a slightly licorice flavor

Birch bark: Woodsy refreshing "root beer"-like taste

Sarsaparilla: Richly fragrant with vanilla-like odor and flavor

Heavenly Flowers Tea

4 parts spearmint

3 parts lemongrass

2 parts hibiscus

1 part rose hips

Infuse for twenty minutes, then add a little honey or sugar.

Inspire-Mint Tea

4 parts rose hips

2 parts chamomile

1 part spearmint

1 part wintergreen

Infuse for twenty minutes, then add a little honey.

Sweet Relaxation

3 parts spearmint

2 parts chamomile

½ part passion flower

½ part rose

¼ part lavender

Infuse for twenty minutes.

Nine

Tools Needed for Scented Oils

There are a few items you will need to use scented oils, either as massage oils or as additions to your herbal spells. You will need to of course buy the essential oils you plan to use; a base of almond, light olive, or jojoba oil for mixing scents; a number of one-or two-ounce brown lidded bottles with labels, rubbing alcohol (do NOT drink) to cleanse your eyedroppers after each use so you don't contaminate other oils; and a small funnel in case you wish to transfer mixed oil from one bottle to another. Three- to six-ounce labeled bottles, or larger, will be needed if you scent your massage oils. If you need to transfer oils from one bottle to another, you will also need a small metal funnel.

When you mix scented oils, add one scent kind at a time to the base oil; gently swirl each oil as it is added. Clean your eyedropper with rubbing alcohol to decontaminate it. Since scented oil mixtures are delicately added drop by drop, I have given the instructions in "parts." The largest "part" will be the primary or base scent, with all other oils contributing their energy as minor notes.

You will find that the uses of oils combined with candles will definitely make a difference in your spell work, as will burning the oils in an aromatherapy diffuser. I strongly advise investing in an aromatherapy diffuser that automatically turns off if the water gets low. This is much safer to use than the traditional ceramic tea light diffuser.

Ten

What Exactly Is Aromatherapy?

Aromatherapy isn't anything new in the healing field. It has been rediscovered from ancient times, when they understood that a person had to be in balance to become totally healed. Aromatherapy is the practice of using scented oils in massage or an aromatherapy burner. A few drops of one or more oils can also be added to a sachet, charm bag, or dry potpourri.

The physical, mental, emotional, and spiritual bodies are very sensitive to odors. Scented oils, according to their uses, affect the mind, emotions, and spirit in specific ways we don't completely understand. We do know that if the entire human layers, or bodies, are not in alignment, the physical body cannot be well. All of these levels are closely connected and must be in coordination to have a healthy, happy life.

When your bodies are aligned, you can better concentrate on your true intent of a spell. You will intuitively know if you are perhaps choosing the wrong spell for a problem or goal.

Massage oils with a few drops of oil added come with some warnings. It is best not to use peanut oil, as some people are highly allergic to peanuts. Other choices are almond, light olive oil, safflower, sunflower, jojoba, coconut, or another natural oil. None of these oils should be ingested, as none of the herbs (except where stated otherwise) should be eaten either. Pregnant women should be extra careful with oils, except when using in an aromatherapy burner.

I also cover the use of candles and oils in this section. The element of fire, signified by the flame, not only destroys, but cleanses and renews. To help you boost your spellwork to a stronger power, I list the color of candles and other information to help you.

When using candles, it is better to use six-inch straights or votive candles. I prefer the votives, as I can put more herbs in the well made by the flame. Since I make my own candles, I deliberately leave a well during making instead of rounding off the top.

Basic Candle Colors

Black: Absorbs and removes anything; reverses, uncrosses, binds negative forces, protects, releases, breaks up blockages, and unsticks stagnant situations. Black also is used to creates confusion and discord among your enemies or repel negative thoughtforms. This color is one of the most powerful available. However, take care that you don't use black for selfish reasons or evil purposes; the energy can backfire upon you.

Blue: The uses of this depends upon the depth of its hue. Light blue is for truth, inspiration, wisdom, protection, understanding, good heal, happiness, inner peace, fidelity, patience, harmony in the home, and contacting the Higher Self. Royal blue is for happiness, loyalty, group success, occult power, and expansion. Use royal blue with caution.

Brown: This color can attract money and financial success and influence earth elementals. It also is helpful for concentration, balance, ESP, intuition, study to fulfill basic material needs, grounding and centering, and to communicate with nature spirits. This color is powerful when used in times of financial crises.

Gold or very clear light yellow: Gold helps with great fortune, intuition, understanding, divination, fast luck (if circumstances are out of your control), and financial benefits. It attracts higher influences, money knowledge, healing, and happiness.

Green: This color is associated with abundance, fertility, good fortune, generosity, material gain, renewal, marriage, balance, healing, and communication with nature spirits. It also can help give a fresh outlook on life or bring balance to an unstable situation.

Indigo: This shade is a Saturn color of such a purplish-blue that it is almost black. It is useful for meditation, and it neutralizes another's magic, balances out karma, and stops another's actions. It is also used to stop gossip, lies, or undesirable competition.

Magenta or Burgundy: This color is a very dark but vibrant red with a deep purple tint to it, like a dark cranberry color. A very high vibrational frequency that tends to make things happen fast, this hue is usually burned with other candles. Burned alone, it is for quick changes, spiritual healing, and exorcism.

Orange: This vibrant color helps with adaptability, encouragement, stimulation, attraction, sudden changes, prosperity, creativity, enthusiasm, success, energy and stamina, and mental agility. It also discourages laziness, helps to gain control, draws good things, and changes luck. As this is a very fast-acting color, be careful and sure you are willing to face major changes.

Pink: Associated with the purest form of true love, friendship, attraction, romance, spiritual awakening and healing, honor, family love, and banishing hatred. This color can also banish depression and negativity.

Purple: This shade helps with success, idealism, higher psychic ability, wisdom, progress, protection, honors, spirit contract, breaking bad luck, driving away evil, divination, greater magickal knowledge, spiritual protection and healing, removing jinxes and hexes, success in court cases, business success, and influencing people who have power over you. Use with caution, for purple is very powerful and the energies difficult to handle.

Red: Associated with energy, strength, sexual potency, physical desire, passionate love, courage, will power, and good health. Also used to protect against psychic attack or conquer fear or laziness.

Silver or very clear light gray: Silver aids with victory, stability, helps with meditation, develops psychic abilities, removes negative powers, neutralizes any situation, and repels destructive forces.

White: This is used for spirituality and greater attainments in life, as well as purity, truth, sincerity, wholeness, power of a higher nature, help with pregnancy and birth, raising vibrations, and destroying destructive energies. When in doubt about a candle color, use white—it is a highly balanced spiritual hue.

Yellow: This brilliant color aids with intellect, imagination, power of the mind, creativity, confidence, gentle persuasion, attraction, concentration, inspiration, mental clarity, knowledge, commerce, medicine, counseling and healing.

Planetary Colors

Candles in these colors can be used on the appropriate days or to call upon certain energy forces. Refer to the Days of the Week section that follows.

Earth: Browns, tans

Jupiter: Royal blue, purples, bright blue

Mars: All shades of red

Mercury: Yellows, orange, yellow-green

Moon: Silver, pink, cream, light gray, white, very light blue

Saturn: Black, very darkest blue, very darkest purple, dark brown

Sun: Gold, orange, deep yellow

Venus: Pink, green, pale blue, all pastel colors

Days of the Week Colors

Candles used to symbolize a day of the week are similar to planetary candles, in that they are burned to invoke a particular planetary energy power.

Sunday—The Sun: Yellow, gold

Monday—The Moon: White, silver, light gray

Tuesday—Mars: Red

Wednesday—Mercury: Purple, yellow

Thursday—Jupiter: Blue

Friday—Venus: Green

Saturday—Saturn: Black, purple

Eleven

Oils for Mental, Emotional, and Spiritual Matters

Magickal oils are primarily used to concentrate the powers of an herb, flower, tree, or root. The greatest value of oils is that they retain the full scent of the plant.

In all traditions, oil is a symbol of the element of Fire. The oils capture, draw out, and store the essential nature of herbs and flowers, basic energies that the old wise ones called the "fiery being."

Oil magick works through vibrations and scent, primarily on the mind, emotions, and spirit—the other layers of our physical body we tend to overlook most of the time. The vibratory rate of an herb, oil, or incense determines whether it is positive or negative, and the degree thereof. All herbal and oil magick works through vibrations. Scents trigger various centers in the brain and bring them into dominance. Thus, lilac oil stimulates the psychic center and helps develop clairvoyant powers. Other centers include the intellectual, spiritual, and so on.

Since the magickal power of perfumes and oils lies in the scent, good synthetic substitutes can be just as powerful as the real thing. Avoid any oils that evolve through animals. The same applies to illegal ivory or animal products.

Acacia: Possessing high spiritual vibrations, this oil is worn to aid meditation and to develop psychic powers. It aids in prayer, atonement, and divination.

Allspice: Enhances the psychic powers and gives added determination and energy.

Almond: Sweet almond oil, the symbol of wakefulness to the ancient Egyptians, is used in rituals (anointing candles, money, etc.) and also added to money incenses. A good carrier oil.

Ambergris: This comes from whales, so buy the synthetic type. Resonates with the highest spiritual energy and promotes the purest love. Clary sage resembles ambergris.

Angelica: May be used to promote the proper atmosphere for meditation, spells, and prayer work. Worn on the self, it protects from evil influences. It is ruled by the Sun, and raises one's own vibrations when worn.

Anise: A boon to clairvoyance, it stimulates the psychic centers and helps in love affairs.

Apple Blossom: Wear to promote happiness and success. Anoint candles during love rituals.

Basil: Creates harmony on all levels.

Bay: A very powerful scent, useful for protection, meditation, visions, divination, exorcism, purification, and power in general.

Bayberry: Can be used for protection and psychic receptivity. Anoint green candles for prosperity in the home. My grandmother loved to have bayberry candles out when family was traveling during the holidays.

Benzoin: Brings peace of mind. However, if burned on incense charcoal, it will make billowing clouds of smoke.

Bergamot: Induces rest and peaceful sleep. Use in protective spells and for drawing prosperity.

Birch: New beginnings. Birch leaf oil is used to anoint special love candles that are burned to protect one's lover and to smooth over romantic difficulties.

Camphor: Wear a drop to strengthen psychic powers. Also anoint yourself when you have decided to break off with a lover, or when they have done so with you and you find it hard to let go.

Carnation: A good power oil. It is stimulating, energy-promoting, and an aid in healing. Wear when extra energy is needed for a spell.

Cedar Leaf (Thuja) or Cedar Wood: These are both oils of Jupiter, and consequently promote peace, contentment, wealth, and good fortune, in addition to driving away all evil and negativity. These oils are believed to attract good spirits and repel bad ones.

Cherry Blossom: Brings peace, harmony, happiness, relaxation, wealth, and good fortune. It is especially good against loneliness.

Cinnamon: A high vibration oil, used for personal protection. Added to any incense, it increases its powers. Mixed with powdered sandalwood, it makes an incense suitable for all religious or spiritual magick. Ruled by the Sun, it is excellent for clairvoyance, healing, wealth, problem solving, meditations, and protection.

Cinquefoil: Protective, strengthens the five senses. Since it also represents the "five lucks" (love, money, health, power, and wisdom), it is often used to anoint amulets and charm bags.

Clove: Good for driving away disease and evil influences.

Coriander: A love oil used to anoint candles.

Cumin Seed: This brings peace and harmony to the home. Anoint all doorways once a week just before sunrise when the household is asleep, and all is quiet.

Cyclamen: Worn to ease childbirth by the expectant mother. Also used in love and marriage spells.

Cypress: An oil of Saturn, it vibrates on a high plane, as all oils of Saturn do. An oil of blessing, consecration, and protection, it brings peace and relaxation, controlling the self-willed. It is a symbol of the Earth element, as well as of death. It also effectively screens out the negative vibrations of funeral mourners. Wear on Halloween (Samhain) to become aware and remember those who have passed on.

Eucalyptus: A healing oil that is very useful in recuperation after a long illness. Burned in an aromatherapy burner, it has the power to purify the air and cut down on colds during the winter season.

Fir: Promotes peace and contentment.

Frangipani: Erotic.

Frankincense: One of the most powerful and sacred of all oils, it is a strong purifier for exorcisms, purification, blessings, meditation, and visions. It vibrates with the highest energy of the Sun and affords great psychic protection.

Gardenia: A highly magnetic oil, excellent for protection and to attract love. It calms and promotes feelings of pure love, as well as being especially good for mental problems.

Ginger: A tropical aphrodisiac that induces passion.

Heliotrope: High spiritual vibrations, drenched with the energies of the Sun. Promotes peace and harmony; aids in clairvoyance, meditation, and psychic development.

High John the Conquer: Use for power, courage, justice. It is a good oil to wear into court.

Honeysuckle: Stimulates the mind and creativity. Also use in love and prosperity spells.

Hyacinth: A very restful vibration. When worn, it gives peace and rest from anxiety. In a sachet bag under your pillow, it promotes sleep as well as psychic dreams.

Hyssop: Increases finances. Added to the bath, it creates a purifying atmosphere.

Jasmine: A purely spiritual oil. This is a lunar oil, a symbol of the Moon, and of the mysteries of the night. It has many occult properties. Use to anoint yourself, candles, and so on. Gives psychic protection, balance, peace, sleep, eases childbirth, and will help attract and hold a lover. Also good for meditation, prayer, psychic sensitivity, and astral projection.

Lavender: Mercury rules this oil, and it can be used to anoint yourself, sacred objects, and many other things. It is a cleansing and purifying oil, so it is good for exorcisms, purification, good health, restful sleep, and peace. A good oil for an aromatherapy burner.

Lemon: Attracts love. Also makes a good room deodorizer.

Lemongrass: An aid to the psychic powers. Will help make contact with spirits.

Lilac: Induces Far Memory, the act of recalling past lives. Is useful in inducing clairvoyant powers in general. Brings peace and harmony. Stimulates mental and creative powers.

Lily of the Valley: This oil is sacred to the Great Goddess, and when worn is soothing to the nerves. The peace it gives is both spiritual and emotional, and it brings the highest of blessings.

Linaloe: An energetic vibration enhancer, it also promotes good health and vitality.

Lotus: The most sacred oil of the ancient Egyptians. A powerful oil, it is sacred to the Moon, the goddess Isis, and magick. It can be worn on the self or used to anoint sacred objects. Good for psychic protection, happiness, good health, fertility, good fortune, peace, harmony, and blessings. It is most beneficial for astral projection and visions. This oil has a high spiritual vibration.

Magnolia: An excellent oil for meditation and psychic development, it also brings peace and harmony.

Melilot: Fights depression, or what was once called melancholy.

Mimosa: Used in healing spells, but also can produce prophetic dreams.

Mint: A very magnetic scent for attracting money and good fortune. Use it to anoint you wallet or purse. Use in prosperity spells, and to increase one's business.

Musk: The universally accepted "sex scent," a magnetic oil worn with equal success by both sexes. This is another animal scent, so use synthetic substitutes. This oil also can be used for courage, determination, and energy.

Myrrh: A very sacred oil with high spiritual vibrations, myrrh is ruled by Saturn and the Great Goddess. It gives powerful protection and is one of the best scents for use in exorcisms, purification, meditation, prayer, and healing. Sweet Cicely smells similar.

Myrtle: Sacred to Venus, this oil has vibrations of love when used in small amounts.

Narcissus: A narcotic type of oil, it is often called the perfume of Persephone. It aids in achieving good health and a harmonious relaxed outlook. It promotes sleep and trance states and can be used for protection.

Neroli: A magnetic women's oil, it can be rubbed between the breasts to attract men. *See Orange Blossom.*

Nutmeg: A bit of this oil on your temples and third eye aids in meditation and prayer. It also promotes sleep.

Orange: Both bitter and sweet orange oils are conducive to finding peace and balanced emotions.

Orange Blossom: Also called Neroli. This oil vibrates with the energy of love and attraction and is reputed to induce proposals of marriage.

Orris Root: Aids concentration, creativity, strengthens determination and desire. Sometimes called "iris."

Patchouli: A very powerful Eastern occult oil. It is magnetically erotic but also can be used for a peaceful separation. Put some on your doors to keep unwanted people away. Wards off negativity and evil, and gives peace of mind.

Peony: A lucky scent for all who need customers, success in business, or good fortune.

Peppermint: Use to create changes within one's life. Also used to relax and allow one to unwind.

Pine: Purifying and deodorizing, this is an oil of Mars. Also excellent for exorcism and defense.

Rose: This is one of the most sacred and powerful of perfumes. It is an oil of Venus that promotes love, beauty, artistic creativity, health, peace, and balance while dispelling anger. Used in all love spells and can be added to baths.

Rose Geranium: Affords psychic protection, and is often used to exorcise and protect a new home by anointing the doors and windowsills. It affords good health, dispels fear, and promotes courage.

Rosemary: One of the most powerful herbs of protection and exorcism. It can be put on the doors and windowsills to purify and bless a house. It attracts peace, health, prudence, common sense, determination, willpower, and courage.

Aids psychic development, helps with prophetic dreams, and protects against nightmares. Can also be used in healing spells.

Rue: Can break up negativity and curses. Add nine drops of this oil to the bath every night for nine nights in succession during the waning Moon to break a spell that has been cast against you. Soak any found magickal image or poppet with this oil and burn the object to break a spell.

Sandalwood: Another very powerful, spiritual fragrance from the East. Raises one's vibrations. Ruled by Mercury and promotes good health, meditation, visions, and protection. It is said to aid in opening the doors to past incarnations.

Sesame: Gives hope to one who is sick, discouraged, or lonely.

Spikenard: Wear during rituals for the ancient deities of Egypt.

Stephanotis: A good oil for the psychic as it aids the will and promotes determination. Also attracts love in a powerful way.

Strawberry: Aids in the acquisition of wealth and good fortune.

Styrax: An oil of Mercury, this oil vibrates on a high plane.

Tuberose: Mistress of the Night, as it is also known, is an excellent aphrodisiac. Promotes peace and also aids in psychic powers. Very much a physical oil.

Vanilla: A vitalizing oil, said to be sexually arousing in women. Use as an energy restorer. Also used to gain extra power during spell work.

Vervain: A very magickal herb used by the Celts for protection and love. Also use to attract material good fortune, to stimulate the mind and intellectual creativity, as well as for exorcism, purification, and general attraction.

Violet: Said to be sacred to the Fairy Queen. Very healing when added to baths. It is another protective perfume, wards off evil, promotes good health, and aids in achieving peace, especially in marital problems. It can also promote reunions and break down the barriers of indifference. Attracts wealth and good fortune.

Wisteria: This oil is a bridge to the higher planes and unlocks the door to the spirit world; the door between the world of men and the realms of the deities, the passport to higher consciousness. It is therefore a very powerful aid to any kind of divination, illumination, astral projection, spirit journeys, or psychic work. It greatly enhances the results of meditation. Wear only when in complete serenity.

Ylang-Ylang: Sometimes call "flower of flowers." Attracts the opposite sex and love. Also soothes the problems of married life. It can help in finding a job by making you calmer and more impressive.

Scent Groups

Intoxicating: Fragrance of flowers (especially narcissus) and balsams; sweet mellow odors; soft quality; relaxing

Non-sexual or Refreshing: Green residue fragrances of saps and leaves of plants, camphor, pine, some mints, citrus oils; healthy clean wake-up quality

Sexually Stimulating: Animal odors, costus root, ambrette seed; slightly rancid-smelling; low and dark quality.

Spicy and Bitter: Seeds, roots, stalks, some leaves. Mosses and woods fall halfway into this category. Some, like santal, share some floral overtones. Businesslike activating quality.

Fixatives: Orris root, oakmoss, reindeer moss, storax, balsam of Peru, balsam of Tolu, benzoin, frankincense, myrrh, musk, ambergris, civet (synthetic only), castorum, costus root, ambrette seed, calamus root, clary sage

Spicy Scents

Allspice berries (also known as pimiento or Jamaica pepper); smells like a mixture of cloves, nutmeg, and cinnamon

Cassia wood, beads, or oil

Cinnamon bark or oil

Cloves

Cubeba (smells a little like mace)

Galangal oil (sweet spicy fragrance; the root itself doesn't have much scent)

Ginger root or oil

Mace blades

Nigella seeds (warm, spicy smell)

Nutmeg

Nutmeg geranium leaves

Sweet and Floral Scents

Acacia flowers

Ambergris oil

Apple blossom oil

Apple mint leaves

Bois de rose oil

Cactus flowers or oil

Calamus root or oil

Campernella oil (smells like jonquil)

Cardamom pods or oil (very aromatic when crushed)

Carnation flowers or oil

Champac oil (a variety of marigold)

Cherry blossom oil

Clove pink flowers or oil

Clover flower oil

Coriander seeds (pungently sweet when crushed)

Frangipani oil

Gardenia oil

Geranium leaves or oil

Guaiac wood oil (rose-like fragrance)

Heliotrope oil (like a mixture of anise, almond, and vanilla)

Honeysuckle flowers or oil

Hyacinth flowers or oil

Jasmine flowers or oil

Lavender flowers or oil

Lily flowers or oil

Lily of the Valley flowers or oil

Linden flowers (*Tilia europaea*, also known as lime flowers)

Lotus flowers or oil

Magnolia flowers or oil

Mignonette flowers (*Reseda odorata*)

Mimosa flowers or oil

Narcissus flowers or oil (also known as jonquil)

Neroli oil

Neroli petal oil

Nicotiana (tobacco) flowers or oil

Orange mint leaves

Orris root or oil

Palmarosa oil (geranium-like fragrance)

Peach blossom oil

Pineapple mint leaves (very good in sachets)

Raspberry leaves or oil (mildly fragrant leaves)

Rosebuds, petals, or oil

Rose geranium leaves (an excellent substitute for rose buds, in some case even more fragrant)

Rosemary leaves or oil

Spike lavender flowers or oil

Strawberry oil

Stephanotis flowers or oil

Sweetbriar leaves

Sweet pea flowers or oil

Syringa oil

Tuberose oil

Tulip flowers or oil

Violet leaves or oil

Wallflower (*Erysimum spp.*) flowers or oil

Wisteria flowers or oil

Yarrow flowers

Ylang-Ylang flowers or oil (very powerful and exotic)

Yucca flowers

Citrus Scents

Balm leaves

Bergamot leaves or oil

Bigarade (bitter or Seville orange peel) oil

Citronella oil

Gas plant (fraxinella, *Dictamnus albus*) leaves

Grapefruit leaves, peel, or flowers

Lemongrass

Lemon leaves, peel, or flowers

Lemon oil (extracted from the peel)

Lemon-scented geranium leaves

Lemon verbena leaves

Lime leaves, peel, or flowers (*Citrus acida*)

Lime oil (extracted from the peel)

Orange leave, peel, or flowers

Orange oil (extracted from the peel)

Petitgrain, oil of (orange leaf oil)

Portugal, oil of (sweet orange peel oil)

Tangerine leaves, peel, flowers

Herby Scents

Angelica root or oil

Anise leaves, seeds, or oil.

Basil leaves or oil (clove-like fragrance)

Calamint leaves

Costmary leaves (mixture of mind and chrysanthemum fragrance)

Dill seed or oil

Dittany of Crete leaves (a little like the smell of dried marjoram)

Fennel seeds or oil

Marjoram leaves or oil (this oil is much more fragrant than the dried leaves)

Oregano leaves or oil

Pennyroyal leaves or oil (somewhere in between peppermint and vanilla)

Peppermint-scented geranium leaves

Peppermint leaves or oil

Perilla leaves (anise-like fragrance)

Sage leaves or oil

Spearmint leaves or oil

Sweet Cicely leaves, seeds or oil (a myrrh-like fragrance)

Tansy leaves

Thyme leaves or oil

Wintergreen leaves or oil

Woodruff leaves (smells like freshly mown hay)

Woodsy Scents

Acacia wood and oil (needs reinforcing by other fragrances)

Almond (sweet) oil

Ambrette seeds (also known as amber and musk seed)

Ambrosia (also known as cheopdium or wormseed; smells a little like eucalyptus)

Balm of Gilead (poplar bush; very sweet, mellow scent)

Bayberry bark or oil

Bay leaves or oil

Birch bark or oil

Brazilwood (nothing really exciting)

Cajeput oil (smells like a delicious combination of rosemary, camphor, and cardamom)

Cascarilla bark

Cedarwood chips, leaves, or oil

Civet oil or tincture (buy synthetic)

Clary sage leaves or oil (smells like balsam of Tolu)

Deer's tongue leaves (strong, vanilla-like fragrance)

Eucalyptus leaves or oil

Frankincense gum or oil

Juniper oil

Labdanum leaves

Mastic gum (must be combined with an oil)

Melilot flowers (smells like tonka or woodruff)

Musk oil or tincture (buy synthetic)

Musk-scented geranium leaves

Myrtle leaves (faint eucalyptus fragrance)

Oakmoss (very woodsy)

Pine needles or oil

Rhodium oil (wood of Rhodes oil)

Sandalwood rasping or oil (white or yellow; red is a
   different wood altogether)

Sassafras wood or oil (spicy and woodsy)

Spruce oil

Sumbul root (also known as musk root; delightful
   musky scent)

Sweet fern (woodsy)

Thus gum (spruce or pine resin; must be combined with an oil)

Tonka beans (vanilla-like aroma)

Vanilla pods or essence

Vetiver (fabulous fragrance like myrrh and sandalwood)

Wormseed—See Ambrosia

Bitter or Pungent Scents

Almond oil, bitter

Caraway seeds or oil

Catnip leaves or oil

Cotton lavender leaves

Cypress leaves, roots or oil

Galbanum, gum (must be combined with an oil)

Hyssop leaves or oil (the oil is more fragrant than the dried leaf)

Life everlasting leaves

Myrrh, gum (must be combined with an oil)

Patchouli leaves or oil (a gorgeous earthy fragrance)

Rue leaves or oil (use carefully)

Santolina leaves (another variety of lavender cotton)

Southernwood leaves (bitter, lemony smell)

Wormwood leaves or oil (bitter)

Fixatives for Sachets and Potpourris

(The general formula for sachets and potpourris is one ounce fixative to every two quarts of herbs)

Ambergris oil or tincture

Balsam of Peru (extremely useful; particularly good for heliotrope, linden, and lotus)

Balsam of Tolu (extremely useful, especially with ambrette, acacia, champak, honeysuckle, magnolia, wall flower, any dry potpourris)

Benzoin gum

Calamus root or oil

Castoreum (smells like Russian leather; buy synthetic)

Cedarwood chips or oil (use sparingly, as it is very powerful)

Civet oil or tincture (buy synthetic)

Clary sage

Lemon peel

Mastic gum

Musk oil or tincture (buy synthetic)

Opopanax gum

Orange peel

Orris root

Patchouli leaves

Sandalwood (useful for any rose mixture)

Sandac gum

Storax gum (also known as stacte)

Sumbul root

Tangerine peel

Thus gum (both spruce and pine resin go by this name
now; frankincense used to have another name)

Useful Incense Gums

A gum is water-soluble, a resin is not. Resins and balsams
(known as oleo-resins, half essential oil and half resin) burn
with a smoky flame and give off their essential oil when
heated. Consequently, for the best effect they have to be
fumed rather than burned. Resins are the chief ingredients
of the incenses of the Catholic and orthodox churches. The
most widely used are frankincense, with myrrh, benzoin,
and galbanum added in lesser amounts, depending on the
grade of incense involved. The best grade, often called "high
altar" incense, is generally pure frankincense alone.

Balsam of Peru (sweet smelling)

Balsam of Tolu (sweet smelling)

Bdellium, gum (an inferior type of myrrh; bitter)

Benzoin gum (very aromatic; there are two varieties:
   Sumatra, sweet and rather like storax, and Siamese,
   which has a vanilla-like fragrance

Camphor, gum (cold and spicy)

Dragon's blood resin (Calamus draco; sweetly pungent)

Frankincense gum or olibanum (a little like lavender;
   exquisite aroma)

Galbanum gum (gorgeously bittersweet)

Mastic gum (a sharp, light aroma)

Myrrh gum (bitter and mysterious)

Sandarac gum (cedar-like)

Storax gum, or stacte (cloyingly sweet)

Thus gum (piney)

Twelve

Creating Special Atmospheres

These formulae for perfumed oils and massage oils can be made in small or large qualities; "small" will yield one to two ounces for personal use or anointing candles; "large" means six to eight ounces for massages. If you want to double-charge your candle spells, choose two or three appropriate herbs, fine-grind them, spread them on a paper towel, and roll the candle over them.

After the essential oils are mixed with the carrier oil, hold the bottle between your hands and focus on the intent you desire. Fill your bottle three-quarters full of carrier oil (almond, jojoba, whatever oil you choose). Then add the required drops of essential oils, (eye droppers are necessary) swirling gently after each addition. Cap and label each bottle. Remember to gently swirl each bottle again just before use.

Each time you use a dropper (unless the oil bottle has its own dropper), you need to flush the dropper with rubbing alcohol. Do this by drawing in and flushing with alcohol several times.

For aromatherapy, blend essential oils without the carrier oil. Drop the oils directly into the water in the container that sits over the heat.

One drop of benzoin as a fixative should go into every bottle of personal magickal oil (at least two drops into the massage oils) to keep them from turning rancid. You can also put in a tiny chip of an appropriate stone.

Personal Oils

Changing Your Luck: 1 drop cedar; 1 drop birch, 3 drops frankincense, 1 drop High John

Cleansing: 3 drops frankincense, 1 drop pine, 2 drops lotus

Happiness: 1 drop strawberry, 3 drops rose

Harmony: 2 drops honeysuckle, 2 drops lilac, 4 drops magnolia

Healing: 1 drop cinnamon, 3 drops myrrh, 1 drop clove

Letting Go: 1 drop cypress, 1 drop pine, 3 drops pine

Money, attracting: 4 drops bayberry, 3 drops bergamot, 1 drop mint

New Job: 1 drop mint, 2 drops violet, 4 drops ylang-ylang

New Venture: 2 drops frankincense, 1 drop birch, 3 drops mint

Optimism: 1 drop cinquefoil, 3 drops lotus, 2 drops orris root

Perfect Mate, finding: 2 drops ambergris, 2 drops gardenia, 2 drops jasmine

Protection: 2 drops bay, 1 drop cinnamon, 2 drops rosemary

Psychic Shield: 3 drops patchouli, 1 drop cinnamon, 1 drop frankincense

Releasing People: 2 drops High John, 2 drops frankincense, 1 drop cinnamon

Rid of Negatives: 4 drops patchouli, 1 drop pine, 1 drop rue

Self-Confidence: 3 drops hyacinth, 3 drops lotus

Serenity: 4 drops lotus, 2 drops lily of the valley

Spirit Guides, attracting: 2 drops honeysuckle, 2 drops lotus, 1 drop sandalwood

Spiritual Growth: 3 drops wisteria, 1 drop lilac, 1 drop lotus, 1 drop heliotrope

Massage Oils

Change Your Luck: 4 drops violet, 2 drops peony, 2 drops High John

Cleansing: 4 drops lavender, 1 drop hyssop, 2 drops lotus

Happiness: 2 drops gardenia, 2 drops honeysuckle, 1 drop rose

Harmony: 1 drop orange, 4 drops magnolia, 1 drop lilac

Healing: 2 drops myrrh, 4 drops lotus, 2 drops mimosa

Letting Go: 2 drops frankincense, 3 drops patchouli, 1 drop cypress

Money, attracting: 1 drop mint, 3 drops bayberry, 2 drops hyssop

New Job: 2 drops ylang-ylang, 1 drop birch, 2 drops violet, 1 drop lotus

New Venture: 1 drop birch, 1 drop mint, 3 drops frankincense

Optimism: 4 drops lily of the valley, 1 drop rose, 2 drops lotus

Perfect Mate, finding: 2 drops ambergris, 3 drops frangipani, 1 drop jasmine, 2 drops musk

Protection: 3 drops frankincense, 3 drops myrrh, 1 drop rosemary

Psychic Shield: 2 drops frankincense, 2 drops myrrh, 3 drops bay

Release People: 2 drops High John, 1 drop pine, 4 drops patchouli

Ridding of Negatives: 3 drops patchouli, 2 drops cinnamon, 2 drops clove

Self-Confidence: 4 drops magnolia, 2 drops, lotus, 1 drop violet

Serenity: 2 drops hyacinth, 3 drops lotus, 2 drops lily of the valley, 1 drop narcissus

Spirit Guides, attracting: 4 drops wisteria, 2 drops sandalwood

Spiritual Growth: 3 drops lotus, 2 drops sandalwood, 2 drops wisteria, 1 drop honeysuckle

Now for some fun and/or tasty ways of using roses.

Rose Ointment

½ cup rose water, at room temperature

¼ cup coconut oil

¼ to ½ ounce beeswax chips. Use the smaller amount for a creamier blend.

6 drops rose essential oil

Melt the coconut oil and beeswax together over low heat. Whip in the rose water and add the essential. Apply to dry skin, lips, hands, and feet.

Rose Petal Infusion

Harvest fresh, unsprayed roses and pack a wide-mouth quart jar with the petals. Do not put in the hips and centers. Fill with water. Put in the refrigerator for a minimum of two hours. Can be warmed for tea or added in small amounts for flavoring.

Rose Cream for Dessert

2 cups whipped cream, canned coconut milk, or yogurt

1 tablespoon honey or sweetener

1 drop rose essential oil

Mix together and serve as a dessert topping.

Rose Honey

½ cup liquid honey

1 drop rose essential oil

Mix well and store in airtight container. Wonderful flavor for tea or toast.

Creams

You can easily make your own facial and body creams in the herbal scents you like best. Go to your local pharmacy and chose an inexpensive, unscented (or scent of your choice) jar of cream that is hypoallergenic. Empty the jar of cream into the top of a double boiler, and heat over boiling water. Put in the herbs you have selected (rose, chamomile, tuberose, violet, et cetera) and simmer very gently for two hours with the lid on the pot. Use about one ounce of dried herbs or two and a half ounces of fresh herbs per ten ounces of cream base. Remove from the heat. Strain though cheesecloth and pack into jars with tight fitting lids. Cool to room temperature before putting on the lids. Seal tightly and keep in a cool, dark place.

Decoction

This is the method of extraction from the toughest plant materials such as roots and bark. Combine the herbs and cold water in a pan. Use about one ounce dried herbs or two ounces fresh herbs per two cups of water. Bring to a boil and simmer gently for twenty to forty minutes, or until the liquid is reduced by half to one-third. Strain the liquid into a container and cover. Store in a cool place or refrigerate. Decoctions are best when freshly made.

Infusion

This is simply brewing a strong tea. Use one tablespoon of fresh herbs or two tablespoons of dried herbs to a cup of water. To make a cold infusion, steep the herbs in cold water overnight in a sealer container. For a hot infusion, steep herbs for ten minutes in a covered container of boiling water. In this last method, remove from the heat as soon as you put in the herbs, and push them down into the water. Place in the sun. Allow the herbs to steep for three to four weeks, gently shaking the jar daily. Strain and bottle.

For a hot oil infusion, combine fresh herbs and sunflower, almond, or light olive oil in the top of a double boiler. Heat over boiling water for two hours with the lid on. Use one cup of fresh herbs per two cups of oil, half a cup of dried herbs. Do not allow the oil to boil. Strain the liquid through cheesecloth, and store in bottles in a cool dark place.

Infused oils can be used for massage, serve as the base for ointments, or even added in cooking.

Syrup for a Sore Throat

1 ⅓ cups water

½ teaspoon mallow

1 tablespoon hyssop

1 cup rose hips

½ teaspoon angelica

½ cup honey

Combine the herbs and water in the top of a double boiler. Heat over boiling water for about twenty minutes or until the rose hips are soft. Press the herbs through a colander and add the honey. Store in a covered container in the refrigerator.

Gargle for a Sore Throat

½ teaspoon grated garlic

2 tablespoons honey

¾ cup warm water

Keeping the water at a very low simmer, heat the mixture for twenty. Strain and bottle.

Clara's Quick Sore Throat Remedy

Add ½ teaspoon of salt to a tall glass of very warm water. Gargle thoroughly with this.

It wasn't just the salt gargle that helped but the way my grandmother taught me to gargle that seemed to make the difference. She explained that the entire throat needed to be cleansed with the salt water. This meant that when you gargled, you needed to stick out your tongue to allow the mixture to get as far down the throat as possible. She was right—it did make a difference.

Chest Rubs for Chest Colds

½ cup basil

¼ cup anise or hyssop

2 cups oil

OR

½ cup mint

½ cup thyme

2 cups oil

Make a hot infusion using the herbs and oil. Massage into the chest area.

CAUTION: Do not use basil or anise during pregnancy.

Herbal Teas or Tisanes

Teas (or tisanes) are made as hot infusions. Do not boil the water after adding the herbs. Pour the hot water over the herbs and cover. Let steep for five to fifteen minutes. Strain.

Headache Tea

2 teaspoons fresh catnip or 1 teaspoon dried catnip

1⅓ cups hot water

Pour the hot water over the herbs, which are in a strainer.

Relaxing Tea

2 teaspoons fresh chamomile or 1 teaspoon dried chamomile

1½ cups boiling water

Pour water over the herbs in a strainer and relax.

Flatulence Tea

1 teaspoon fennel

1 teaspoon anise

1½ cups boiling water

Pour the water over the herbs and strain.

Digestive Tea

1 teaspoon fresh mint

1 teaspoon fresh bee balm

1½ cups boiling water

Make an infusion using the method above. This helps with digestion.

Homemade Rose Water

This can be applied to the face as a liquid or used as a liquid base to make a cream or salve. Place one cup chopped or shredded fresh rose petals in two cups cold water, stir well. Let stand, covered, overnight. If possible, use a heavy glass weight to keep the petals under the water. Strain and pour the liquid into a clean jar. Pierce a vitamin E capsule, adding that to the jar as a preservative. Keep refrigerated.

Acne and Pimples

Keep your skin extremely clean, watch what you eat, and dab pharmacy-brand witch hazel on the acne or pimples.

Oily Skin

Mix ½ half cup apple juice and two teaspoons witch hazel. Apply to clean face with cotton balls.

Hair Care

For dandruff, mix equal parts vinegar and water, and use as a final hair rinse. Do not rinse this out of your hair.

For dry hair, apply just-warmed unsaturated oil to your hair. Cover with plastic, and cover the plastic with a soft towel. Leave in for half an hour to two hours, then shampoo. You also can use an herb-infused oil on your hair: sage and rosemary for dark hair, chamomile for fair.

Cider Tonic

Helps with digestion, morning sickness, pain of sinusitis or arthritis, and reduces high blood alkalinity (chronic fatigue).

1 large glass water

1 teaspoon cider vinegar

1 teaspoon honey

Mix well and drink.

Night Time Sachet

These are put under the pillows. Personally, I spritz the fresh sheets on the bed with lavender water. To make a sachet, use an old nylon stocking for the herbs and tie the ends shut tightly.

2 parts hop flowers

4 parts rose petals

½ part woodruff flowers

½ part lavender buds

1 part lady's mantle, leaves and flowers

Mix the herbs. Tie one end the stocking about four inches from the toe. Stuff in the herbs, and tie the other end tightly closed. Place between the pillow and pillowcase.

Athlete's Foot

Keep the feet (especially between the toes) very clean and dry. My father swore that wearing white socks helped. He also used to pour Absorbine Jr. over his toes to kill athlete's foot. This procedure stung so badly that he accompanied it with loud commentary.

Honey is very useful in herbal formulae and to body skin cleansing. Honey is a natural rejuvenator and antibiotic. Skin ages not because it loses its ability to hold oil, but because it loses its ability to hold moisture. Because honey is acidic, it also help rid the face of blemishes and blackheads.

Honey Ointment for Hands and Arms

Honey is antibacterial and also pulls moisture to the skin.

1 ounce beeswax

1 cup apricot, almond, or light olive oil

Optional: Up to sixty drops essential oils of rose geranium or orange-scented bergamot

Melt the beeswax in the top of a double boiler. Stir frequently to help the melting. This will take about ten minutes. Granular beeswax is easiest to use. Add the cup of oil to the beeswax and stir until well blended. Remove from the heat and cool slightly. Add the essential oils, stirring until well mixed. Pour into jars and label. Don't cap the jars until the mixture is room temperature. Store at room temperature. Spoon onto hands and arms before bed.

Honey Pat

Dip your fingers into a little honey and apply it to your face in an upward revolving motion. Pat with your fingertips as if typing. When it gets so tacky that you fingers stick to your face, stop and rinse gently with warm water.

Age Spots

This is a very old formula for "curing" age spots. It also can be used to prevent bruising if put immediately on the bruise.

1 teaspoon freshly squeezed onion

2 teaspoons apple cider vinegar

Mix together and pat on the age spots on your hands and arms.

Basic Face and Hand Cream

1 ounce lanolin

2 ounces almond oil

½ ounce beeswax

2 ounces soy oil

1 ounce rose water

3 drops essential oil of rose

Melt the lanolin and beeswax in the top of a double boiler. Add the oils, a little a time, stirring constantly. Turn off the head; remove the top of the double boiler from over the boiling water. Slowly add the rose water and essential oil, stirring until the cream was cooled. Pour into amber colored six-ounce jars with lids.

Chapped Skin Lotion

1 tablespoon borax

3 ounces glycerin

12 ounce double rose water

5 5tablespoons mucilage of quince

Shake borax and rosewater together until the borax is dissolved. Add the mucilage of quince to the glycerin and shake together thoroughly. Mix the two solutions together until well blended.

Stomachache

A weak tea of chamomile is good, even for small children, for stomachache, indigestion, colic, gas, and summer diarrhea.

Anti-Flu Remedy

2 teaspoons cayenne pepper

1 cup boiling water

1½ teaspoons sea salt

1 cup apple cider vinegar

Grind the cayenne and salt together to make a paste. Add boiling water or very strong strained chamomile tea. Steep and cool. Add the vinegar. Adults can take a teaspoon to a tablespoon every half hour. If it is too strong, dilute it.

Heart Cordial

Also good for exhaustion, nervous heart trouble, congestion of the liver, headaches, and as a diuretic. Add rosemary to wine of your preference to strengthen the heart and prevent swelling of the ankles. Steep, turn, and shake the herb in the sherry or wine for at least a week, then strain out the rosemary.

Hair Care

Rosemary can be added to shampoos and rinses to prevent dandruff and to strengthen the hair. This is especially good for dark hair.

Sore Throat

Thyme tea laced with honey is effective in fighting sore throats and post-nasal drip. Take a tablespoon several times a day.

Barley Waters

Use this formula to help invalids who find it difficult to eat and to alleviate diarrhea in young children. NOTE: Do not give honey to children under two years of age.

4 ounces whole barley

½ of a lemon peeled, washed

2 ounces honey

Add one pint of water to the barley and lemon peel. Simmer until soft. Remove from the heat and steep. Remove the peel and add the honey.

Lip Balm

2 to 4 teaspoons rose or marigold petals

1 cup almond oil

Fill a jar with the petals, and then pour the oil over them. Close the jar and leave in the sun for five days in summer, fifteen days in winter. Strain using cheesecloth for all the oil.

Warm Rose Oil

1 teaspoon vanilla extract

1 tablespoon beeswax

1 teaspoon vitamin E oil

1 teaspoon honey

1 teaspoon aloe vera gel

Warm the oil in a double boiler. Stir in the beeswax and other ingredients. While hot, pour into a wide-mouth container. Close the lid. The ointment will soon harden.

Liniment #1

1 pint apple cider vinegar

1 teaspoon cayenne pepper

6 drops oil of pine

Check for skin sensitivity. Mix together in a bottle; shake before each use. Useful for sprains, swollen joints, arthritic pain.

Eye Makeup Remover

1 tablespoon canola oil

1 tablespoon light olive oil

1 tablespoon castor oil (drug store)

Mix together and pour into a clean 1½-ounce bottle. To use, put a small amount onto a clean cotton pad and gently wipe over the eyelids.

Chapped Lips

½ teaspoon honey or glycerin

½ teaspoon castor oil

½ teaspoon fresh lemon juice

This recipe has come down through generations. The Midwest, where my grandmother lived for many years, is extremely harsh and cold in winter.

Mix all the ingredients; shore in a ½ ounce jar in the refrigerator. Put it on your lips and leave overnight.

Nail and Cuticle Oil

1 teaspoon jojoba oil

½ teaspoon vitamin E oil

1 teaspoon almond oil

Shake the ingredients together in a small bottle. Soak your nails in warm water for ten minutes, then rub this oil into the nails and cuticles.

Calendula Oil Salve

1 cup calendula oil

4–6 drops lavender essential oil

¼ grated beeswax (optional) pinch of turmeric for coloring

Warm the oil over very low heat and stir in the beeswax. If you want a softer salve, add more oil. Stir in the turmeric.

Pour into small jars or tins. Store in a cool, dark place where it will keep for a year. Apply small amounts to treat skin rashes, wounds, cuts, diaper rash, or cradle cap.

Brain Power Seasoning

3 parts sesame seeds

1 part lecithin granules

4 parts nutritional yeast

1 part spirulina

2 parts powdered kelp

¼ part powdered rosemary

1 part powdered ginkgo

⅛ part each thyme and garlic

1 part powdered gotu kola

Toast the seeds in a heavy skillet; grind them in a seed mill. Combine the seeds with the remaining ingredients. Sprinkle on salads, popcorn, soups, or any main dish.

Bay Rum Aftershave

Bay leaves (fresh if possible)

Ground or grated allspice

Whole cloves

Grated ginger

Rum

Pack a wide-mouth jar with bay leaves, leaving some space at the top. Add the allspice, cloves and ginger. Pour enough rum into the jar to cover the herbs. Cover tightly and let sit for 3 to 4 weeks in a warm place. Strain out the herbs and rebottle the liquid. Add a drop or two of bay essential oil to strengthen the scent.

Cystitis (UTI) Remedy

2 parts cleavers

1 part chickweed

2 parts fresh or dried cranberries

2 parts uva ursi (bearberry)

Combine and prepare as a strong tea. Drink four cups daily, ¼ cup at a time. Drink as much cranberry juice as you can.

Headache Tea

2 parts lemon balm

1 part lavender

1 part feverfew

Combine the herbs and prepare as a strong tea. Drink ¼ cup every thirty minutes until the headache is gone.

Nervous Headache Tea

3 parts chamomile

1 part passionflower

3 parts lemon balm

1 part skullcap

Combine and make a strong infusion tea. Drink ½ cup every hour until the symptoms stop.

Thirteen

Some Final Words

When I look back over the years with my grandmother and three great aunts, I am still amazed at the strong psychic abilities and the little magicks they did with no questions or raised eyebrows from anyone. Great Aunt Leta set a candle in the window over the Winter Solstice holidays to "guide our lost loved ones home for the holidays." Great Aunt Glade, still wearing her corset at age one hundred, seemed to know ahead when she would get visitors. And my grandmother talked to her deceased youngest sister who often appeared at the foot of her bed. Except for my father's dowsing abilities, the psychic traits seem to have skipped a generation. Even then, the families of my two paternal aunts and uncle showed no talents—just my father's children.

Even my mother had death warnings of those within her family during World War II. Goddess knows, nearly all the men in the extended two families and one aunt were in the military during that time. Aunt Viola, my favorite aunt, was killed over Northern California co-piloting a B52 bomber that came in for repairs. We lost no one else, but had a few wounded.

We weren't any monetarily rich family, far from it. We were rich in psychic abilities though. One night when I read tarot cards for my mother, I missed laying out the possible future card, and my mind froze. I knew she had no future. The rest of the cards said her death would come in a few years, and it did. She passed over in her sleep.

I am thankful that I inherited my psychic traits from the Corbin and Smith families and had the opportunity to see this family accept them as normal. My ancestors set my feet on the path I follow today.

Fourteen

Some Books of Interest

This is just a short list. There are hundreds of books on herbs and oils on the market.

Abadie, M. J. *The Everything Herbal Remedies Book.* Holbrook, MA: Adams Media, 2000.

Buchman, Dian Dincin. *Herbal Medicine: The Natural Way to Get Well and Stay Well.* New York: Wings Books, 1979.

Cech, Richo. *Making Plant Medicine.* Williams, OR: Horizon Herbs, 2000.

Cooksley, Valereie Gennari. *Aromatherapy: A Lifetime Guide to Healing with Essential Oils.* Paramus, NJ: Prentice Hall, 1996.

Dodt, Colleen K. *The Essential Oils Book: Creating Personal Blends for Mind & Body.* North Adams, MA: Storey Publishing: 1996.

Gerard, John; revised by Thomas Johnson. *The Herbal or General History of Plants.* New York: Dover Publications, 1975. Originally published 1633.

Gladstar, Rosemary. *Herbal Recipes for Vibrant Health: 175 Teas, Tonics, Oils, Salves, Tinctures, and Other Natural Remedies for the Entire Family.* North Adams, MA: Storey Publishing, 2001.

Grieve, Margaret. *A Modern Herbal.* New York: Dover Publications, 1971.

Hartung, Tammi. *Homegrown Herbs: A Complete Guide to Growing, Using, and Enjoying More Than 100 Herbs.* North Adams, MA: Storey Publishing, 2011.

Kowalchick, Claire, and William H. Hylton, editors. *Rodale's Illustrated Encyclopedia of Herbs.* Emmaus, PA: Rodale Press, 1998.

Leyel, C. F. *Herbal Delights: Tisanes, Syrups, Confections, Electuaries, Robs, Juleps, Vinegars, and Conserves.* New York: Gramercy Publishing, 1986. Originally published 1938.

Pursell, J. J. *The Herbal Apothecary: 100 Medicinal Herbs and How to Use Them.* Portland, OR: Timber Press, 2015.

Rose, Jeanne. *Herbs & Things: A Compendium of Practical and Exotic Lore.* New York: Grosset and Dunlap, 1972.

Tilgner, Sharol. *Herbal Medicine: From the Heart of the Earth.* Pleasant Hill, OR: Wise Acres, 2009.

Tisserand, Robert. *The Art of Aromatherapy: The Healing and Beautifying Properties of the Essential Oils of Flowers and Herbs.* Rochester, VT: Healing Arts Press, 1977.

Worwood, Valerie Ann. *The Complete Book of Essential Oils and Aromatherapy: Over 600 Natural, Non-Toxic and Fragrant Recipes to Create Health, Beauty, a Safe Home Environment.* Novato, CA: New World Library, 1991.

ed
corn Horn
x Dolls
tches Aspirin
tches Bells
tch Grass
tch Herb
tchwood
tches Briar
lf's Claw
lf's Foot
t's Tail

The Magic
: Bay, Palm, Walnut,
g in sap or having

---

in it, as the scent of rose is highly pleasing to the gods. Used in
all love operations and added to baths.

Rose Geranium — Affords psychic protection, and is often used to
exorcise and protect a new home by anointing the door and win
sills. Is also put on the incense burner. It affords good health,
dispels fear, and promotes courage.

Rosemary — One of the most powerful herbs of protection and
exorcism. It can be put on door and window sills as an anointing oil for other objec
bless a house, and is used as an anointing oil to purify a
It attracts peace, health, prudence, commonsense, determinat
willpower, and courage. Aids psychic development, and anoint
the pillow induces prophetic dreams and protects against ni
mares. Is also protective and used in healing rituals.

Rue — To break up negativity and curses, anoint a sprig of da
rue with this oil. Tie up in red bag and carry for protectio
Add 9 drops of this oil to the bath every night for 9 night
succession during the waning Moon to break a spell that
been cast against you. Salt may be added to the bath as
soak any found magical image or poppet with this an
Is an excellent personal protection oil, but sometimes set
violent allergic reactions in people.

Saffron — Wear to aid in the development of clairvoyant p
raises one's vibrations and is excellent for anointing o

Sandalwood — Another very powerful and spiritual fragr
the altar, and ritual objects. Ruled by Mercury and pro
good health, meditation, visions, and protection. Try anointing t
open the doors to past incarnations.
to promote the Sight.

Sesame — Gives hope to one who is sick, discouraged
Egypt, also to anoint sacred objects, such as altars,

Spikenard — Wear during rituals to the ancient deit

Stephanotis — A good oil for the shy as it aids the u
promotes determination. Also attracts love in a powe

Strawberry — Aids in the acquisition of wealth and

Additional Essential Oils

Allspice – adds a pungent note to blends.
Almond, Bitter – scent of freshly baked macaro
Angelica Seed – gives a fresh peppery scent.
Apple Blossom – symbol of perpetual concord; ha
 wafting effect; long lasting.
ay – tree sacred to Apollo; its leaves the sym
 spicy and pleasant with a sweet balsamic
 well with carnation, citrus, and other spice
fberry – spicy, pungent and woody.
rgamot – comes from Italian bitter oranges. Has a rich, sweet
 and fruity aroma.
ch – reminiscent of root beer.
ueberry – sweet and fruity.
deput – has a camphor-like odor.
rnation – Greek legends link it with the goddess Venus and the
 warrior Ajax. Has a clear, spicy aroma which blends well with
 rose, lily of the valley, narcissus, lavender, ylang-ylang, clary
 sage and clove.
darwood – its scent is pleasant, sweet and woody with a smoky
 note. Adds interest to violet, vetiver, patchouli and sandalwood.
ristmas Pine – tangy scent of Christmas.
namon Bark – a strong, spicy, woody aroma. Lends power and
 sweetness.
ronella – pungent and citrusy. Use sparingly.
ry Sage – has a musky scent which was popular in the 17th and
 18th centuries. An excellent fixative for woodsy perfumes; florals
 such as muguet, jasmine, lavender, citrus blends.
e – adds spicy note to florals such as carnation and geranium.
 lso of interest with citrus and cinnamon.
berry – strong, tart and fruity.
ess – sweet balsamic, refreshing aroma. Fixative in woodsy –

---

al fires and for
aditionally made
holly, hawthorn, fir
d, for it will result
ns and pyromancy
of juniper, cedar,

are made from the
moon magic, as
ining water, and ha
d of sacred trees is
lismans, altars,

Pages from the Herbal

What follows is a selection
of pages from D. J.'s herbal.

Table of Weights and Measures, Their Abbreviations and Equivalents

Old Apothecary Symbols and Abbreviations:

t = teaspoon
T = tablespoon
C = cup
cc = cubic centimeter
3 dr = drachm or dram
℥ fl dr = fluid drachm or dram
℥ fl oz = fluid ounce
' ft = foot or feet
g = gram or grains

gr = grains or grain
" in = inch
℈ min = minim
℥ oz = ounce
O. pt = pint
qt = quart
lb = pound
℈ sc = scruple

	SOLID	FLUID
Grain	= 1/20 scruple	
a few grains	= less than 1/8 teaspoon	= 5 drops or minims
15 grains	= 1/4 teaspoon	= 15 drops or minims
20 grains	= 1 scruple or 1/3 dram or 1/3 teasp.	= 20 drops or minims
60 grains	= 1 teaspoon or 1 dram + or 3 scruples	= 60 drops or minims or 1 fluidram
Scruple	= 20 grains or 1/3 dram or 1/3 teasp.	= 20 drops or minims
3 scruples	= 60 grains or 1 teasp. or 1 gram	= 60 drops or minim or 1 fluidram
Pennyweight	= 24 grains or 1/20 ounce	= 24 drops or minim
Dram	= 3 scruples or 1 teaspoon or 60 grains	= 60 drops or minims or 1 fluidram
Teaspoon	= 1/3 tablespoon or 1 dram or 60 grains or 5 grams or 3 scruples	= 60 drops or minims or 1 fluidram
2 teaspoons	= 1 dessertspoon or 2 drams	= 120 drops or minims or 2 fluidrams

Leo. Masc. Heart, sides, upper portion of back. Sun. Rules (1) many plants also ruled by the sun: chamomile, celandine, European angelica, eyebright, marigold, orange, rue, saffron; (2) others: borage, bugloss, peony, poppy.

Virgo. Fem. Solar plexis, bowels. Mercury. Dedicated to Ceres, the Roman goddess of agriculture, and thus rules the cereal plants — oats, barley, rye, wheat — and grasses and sedges.

Libra. Masc. Kidneys, loin, ovaries, low portion of back. Venus. Rules (1) many of the plants also governed by Venus: apple, cherry, primrose, strawberry, white rose, violet.

Scorpio. Fem. Bladder, sex organs. Mars. (1) As the ruler of the sex organs, governs plants that could be considered phallic symbols, such as palms, flowers like calla lilies; (2) others: basil, bramble, wormwood — all plants that are also ruled by Mars.

Sagittarius. Masc. Liver, hips, thighs, condition of the blood. Jupiter. (1) As the centaur and ruler of the forests, rules forest trees with catkins: oak, beech, elm; (2) others: mallows, feverfew.

Capricorn. Fem. Knees, spleen. Saturn. Rules comfrey, cypress, hemlock, nightshades, yew — plants that are also governed by Saturn.

Aquarius. Masc. Calves, ankles, distribution of body fluids. Uranus. Rules frankincense, myrrh.

Pisces. Fem. Feet, psychic faculty. Neptune. As the fishes, rules algae, seaweed, and water mosses.

Moon — cold, fem. — Water
Sun — hot, masc. — Fire
Mercury — cold, sexless? — Earth/Air
Venus — cold, fem. — Earth/Air
Mars — hot, masc. — Fire/Water
Jupiter — hot, masc. — Fire/Water
Saturn — cold, masc. — Earth

Service (Amelanchier species)

Folk Names: Sorb-Apple, Serviceberry
Gender: Cold
Planet: Saturn
Element: Earth
Assoc. Deities: Nephthys, Isis, Demeter, Ceres, Hecate
Parts Used: Fruit
Basic Powers: Knowledge, Reincarnation, Fertility
Specific Uses: Sacred to the Goddess and symbolizes immortality and death and resurrection. Was sacred in the most ancient times and is associated with paleolithic fertility goddesses.

Slippery Elm (Ulmus fulva)

Folk Names: Red Elm, Moose Elm, Indian Elm
Gender: Cold
Planet: Saturn
Element: Earth
Assoc. Deities: Saturn, Isis, Hecate
Parts Used: Leaves, bark
Basic Powers: Protection
Specific Uses: Burn and use in charm bags to stop others from gossiping about you or your friends.

Snapdragon (Antirrhinum majus)

Gender: Cold
Planet: Venus
Element: Fire
Assoc. Deities: Venus, Aphrodite, Hathor, Freya
Parts Used: Flowers, leaves
Basic Powers: Protection
Specific Uses: Flowers are a powerful antidote to witchcraft and black magic. Wear as a protective amulet, or put vases of snapdragons in the house if you feel threatened. Carry with you to see through other people's deceit. Can also be used to counteract charms and spells laid by others by adding to incenses and oil mixtures.

anxieties, is rejuvenative and protective. An excellent all purpose purification and anointing oil can be made by combining sandalwood and rose oils. Similarly, a very effective lustral water for use during exorcisms is rosewater plus sandalwood. Add to healing incenses and burn as a good purifying agent in any room. Also used in making healing oils and incenses. Red sandalwood (Pterocarpus santalinus and S. rubrum) is a different tree, sacred to Venus.

Satyrion
Specific Uses: Possibly vervain, with a root shaped like the male sexual organ; used in potions for love and potency.

Satyrion (Orchis species)
Folk Names: Orchid, Satyr Orchid
Gender: Cold
Planet: Venus
Element: Air
Assoc. Deities: Aphrodite, Astarte, Freya, Hathor
Parts Used: Root
Basic Powers: Love
Specific Uses: Root is used as a powerful aphrodisiac and ingredient of numerous love charms and philtres. The old witches are supposed to have used fresh roots in spells to make love grow, and withered roots in charms to destroy love. The name comes from the belief that it is the favorite food of Satyrs, inciting them to excess.

Scammony (Convolvulus sepium)
Folk Names: Greater Bindweed Root, Hedge Bindweed, Devil's Vine, Hedge Lily, Lady's Nightcap
Gender: Cold
Planet: Saturn
Element: Earth
Assoc. Deities: Saturn, Kronos
Parts Used: Resin, flowering plant, rootstock
Basic Powers: Harvests, Success
Specific Uses: Incenses only

and early July. British Herb Tobacco for relief of asthma and bronchitis: coltsfoot predominantly, plus buckbean, eyebright, betony, rosemary, thyme, lavender, and chamomile.

Comfrey (Symphytum officinale)

Folk Names: Yalluc, Slippery Root, Boneset, Assear, Consolida, Healing Herb, Gum Plant, Consound, Bruisewort, Knitbone, Wallwort, Black Wort, Healing Blade, Salsify
Gender: Cold
Planet: Saturn
Element: Air
Assoc. Deities: Nephthys, Isis, Demeter, Hecate
Parts Used: The herb, root
Basic Powers: Protection
Specific Uses: To ensure your safety while traveling carry some. Put in luggage to ensure its safety.

Copal Gum (Copalquahuitl)

Gender: Hot
Planet: Jupiter
Element: Fire/Water
Assoc. Deities: Jupiter, Zeus, Ra, Osiris
Parts Used: Resin
Basic Powers: Prosperity
Specific Uses: Of Mexican origin, a fragrant, translucent white resin distilled from Copalquahuitl, Mexican Copalli incense. Originally found in Mexico, but is now found in Zanzibar, West Africa, Mozambique Madagascar, and India.

Coriander (Coriandrum sativum)

Folk Names: Cilentro, Cilantro, Culantro, Chinese Parsley
Gender: Hot
Planet: Mars
Element: Fire
Assoc. Deities: Tiw, Horus
Parts Used: Seeds
Basic Powers: Love

Specific Uses: Long used in love sachets and charms. The seeds become very fragrant upon drying and are used in perfumery and incense; the longer they are kept, the more aromatic they become. The Chinese believe they confer immortality.

Costmary (Tanacetum balsamita)

Folk Names: Alecost, Balsam Herb, Herbe Sainte-Marie
Gender: Hot
Planet: Jupiter
Element: Fire/Water
Assoc. Deities: Jupiter, Ra, Zeus, Osiris
Parts Used: Leaves
Basic Powers: Prosperity, Success
Specific Uses: Leaves have a soft balsamic odor and are used in sachets.

Cowslip (Primula veris)

Folk Names: Marsh Marigold, Water Dragon, Palsywort
Gender: Cold
Planet: Venus
Element: Earth/Air
Assoc. Deities: Astarte, Freya, Hathor, Brigid
Parts Used: Flowers
Basic Powers: Visions, Love
Specific Uses: Cowslip wine is slightly narcotic, so perhaps it gives visions of the Goddess. This herb will admit one to Freya's pleasure palace (the pendant flowers suggest a bunch of keys).

Cubeb (Piper cubeba)

Folk Names: Java Pepper, Tailed Pepper
Gender: Hot
Planet: Mars
Element: Fire
Assoc. Deities: Horus, Ares, Tiw
Parts Used: Unripe fruit
Basic Powers: Protection, Physical Attraction
Specific Uses: The dried unripe fruit are burned in incense to drive away evil spirits and carried with one to melt the heart of even

WICCAN NAME	COMMON NAME
Toad	Toadflax
Unicorn Horn	True Unicorn Root
Wax Dolls	Fumitory
Witches Aspirin	White Willow Bark
Witches Bells	Foxglove
Witch Grass	Dog Grass
Witch Herb	Mugwort
Witchwood	Rowan
Witches Briar	Brier Hip
Wolf's Claw	Lycopodium
Wolf's Foot	Bugle Weed
Rat's Tail	Cat Tail

The Magic of Trees

<u>Sun</u>: Bay, Palm, Walnut, Ash, Citrus. <u>Moon</u>: Willow, Ash, trees abounding in sap or having an affinity with water. <u>Mars</u>: Pine, Hawthorn, those that are prickly and thorny. <u>Mercury</u>: Nut-bearing trees (not necessarily edible), Myrtle, Pomegranate, Hazelnut, Mulberry. <u>Jupiter</u>: Birch, Vines, Fig, Oak, Olive, Lime, Maple, Fir. <u>Venus</u>: Apple, Fig, Elder, Plum, Peach, Alder, Birch, Pear, Sycamore. <u>Saturn</u>: Pine, Yew, Elm, Beech, Cyprus, Ivy, Poplar, Quince.

The wood of sacred trees is used in ritual fires and for magic wands of power. Sabbath needfires are traditionally made of nine woods: oak, ash, cherry, rowan, birch, holly, hawthorn, fir, and pine. Elder and willow are never burned, for it will result in very bad luck. A special fire for visions and pyromancy is called the Fire of Azrael and is composed of juniper, cedar, and sandalwood.

Magic wands for various purposes are made from the branches of sacred trees. Willow wands are for moon magic, ash or oak wands for solar magic, hazel for divining water, and hazel or hawthorn for general magic. The wood of sacred trees is also used for pentacles, knife handles, talismans, altars, statues, and other ritual objects. Branches, leaves, and flowers can also

Sunday is ruled by the Sun.
Monday is ruled by the Moon.
Tuesday is ruled by Mars.
Wednesday is ruled by Mercury.
Thursday is ruled by Jupiter.
Friday is ruled by Venus.
Saturday is ruled by Saturn.

The Sun rules all operations involving employers, promotion, friendships, healing, divine power, labor, world leaders.
The Moon rules spells dealing with the home, family, agriculture, cooking, clairvoyance, medicine, dreams, the sea.
Mars rules all operations of conflict, hunting, surgery, lust, physical strength, courage, politics, debates, athletics, war, contests, competitions and rituals involving men.
Mercury rules sites involving studying, learning, teaching, divination, predictions, self-improvement, communications of every kind, the mind, celibacy.
Jupiter rules all rituals of wealth, poverty, monetary matters, legal matters, honors, luck, materialism, expansion.
Venus rules all operations of love, pleasure, art, music, incense and perfume composition, partnerships, rituals involving women.
Saturn rules those operations concerning buildings, the elderly, minerals, wills, reincarnation, destroying diseases and pests, terminations and death.

Raw Materials and Correspondences

Agrimony to Saturn; Bay to the Sun, sometimes Jupiter; Euphorbia to Mars; Eyebright to the Sun, occasionally to Venus or Mercury; Fennel to Mercury, occasionally the Moon; Galangal Root to Jupiter, some authorities say Mars; Grains of Paradise to Jupiter; Lavender to Jupiter, though sometimes to Mercury; Marjoram to Mercury; Oak to Jupiter, sometimes to the Sun; Orris to the Sun, sometimes Jupiter; Peppermint to Venus, sometimes to the Moon; Rhus Aromatica mainly to Mercury;

coltsfoot, water mint.

Herbal Highs

Read Legal Highs and Herbal Highs. You could be exposing yourself to some degree of risk otherwise. It should also be kept in mind that other herbs have quite exotic effects. Such ones as mistletoe, bittersweet, dogwood, vervain, galangal, saffron, black cohosh and the like have just not been absorbed into the herbal mainstream as yet. Herbs are mild and balanced versus heavy and concentrated. It takes sensitive people to appreciate Nature's wonders. ALL herbal highs can be DANGEROUS if abused.

Broom: produces relaxed feelings. Relaxation is deepest during first 2 hours and is followed by mental alertness and increased awareness of color without hallucinations. VERY DANGEROUS.

Calamus: produces stimulation and buoyant feelings. A mind-alterant and hallucinogen.

Catnip: leaves are smoked and produce a mild marijuana-like euphoria, more tense and longer-lasting with tobacco.

Damiana: steeped in hot water or smoked or both. Famous as an aphrodisiac. Has a mild euphoriant effect.

Guarana: stimulant and mood-changer, however, long-term excessive use of caffeine may cause nervousness, insomnia, habituation.

Juniper Berries: the leaves and branches are burnt and the smoke inhaled according to traditional use. Said to be an intoxicant, hallucinogen and deliriant. Duration is about 30 minutes. Possible vision, perhaps of supernatural entities. Not recommended for frequent usage.

Kava Kava: widely used for centuries in Polynesia. Made as a tea, it becomes a mildly stimulating tonic (also an aphrodisiac). Quite different results occur when the root is chewed or extracted. Becomes a powerful euphoriant.

Lobelia: may be smoked or steeped. When smoked, produces mild euphoria, heightened mental clarity, sometimes visual sensations. As a tea, small amounts stimulate, larger ones relax and usually result

Additional Essential Oils

Allspice — adds a pungent note to blends.

Almond, Bitter — scent of freshly baked macaroons.

Angelica Seed — gives a fresh peppery scent.

Apple Blossom — symbol of perpetual concord; has a sweet and gentle wafting effect; long lasting.

Bay — tree sacred to Apollo; its leaves the symbol of victory. Spicy and pleasant with a sweet balsamic undertone. Blends well with carnation, citrus, and other spices.

Bayberry — spicy, pungent and woodsy.

Bergamot — comes from Italian bitter oranges. Has a rich, sweet and fruity aroma.

Birch — reminiscent of root beer.

Blueberry — sweet and fruity.

Cajeput — has a camphor-like odor.

Carnation — Greek legends link it with the goddess Venus and the warrior Ajax. Has a clear, spicy aroma which blends well with rose, lily of the valley, narcissus, lavender, ylang-ylang, clary sage and clove.

Cedarwood — its scent is pleasant, sweet and woody with a smoky note. Adds interest to violet, vetiver, patchouli and sandalwood.

Christmas Pine — tangy scent of Christmas.

Cinnamon Bark — a strong, spicy, woody aroma. Lends power and sweetness.

Citronella — pungent and citrusy. Use sparingly.

Clary Sage — has a musky scent which was popular in the 17th and 18th centuries. An excellent fixative for woodsy perfumes; florals such as muguet, jasmine, lavender, citrus blends.

Clove — adds spicy note to florals such as carnation and geranium. Also of interest with citrus and cinnamon.

Cranberry — strong, tart and fruity.

Cypress — sweet balsamic, refreshing aroma. Fixative in woodsy-type perfumes, as it blends well with cedar, sandalwood, labdanum, the citruses.

valuable medicine and cosmetic, internally and externally. The leaves, bark, and young twigs are astringent, tonic, cleansing, styptic, and sedative.

Woodbase

Specific Uses: Sawdust. Can be used in many incenses. Woods have the same planetary rulerships as the more expensive ingredients. Soft woods come under the Moon and Venus; hard woods under Mars and Saturn; "redwoods" for Mars; expensive and rare woods for the Sun and Jupiter; genuine Rosewoods under Venus; the "blackwoods" under Saturn; walnut to the Sun; the commonly called "yellow-woods" for Mercury and the Sun; "white or cream-woods," e.g. Ash, under the Moon.

Woodruff (Asperula odorata)

Folk Names: Sweet Woodruff, Master of the Woods, Woodrove, Wuderove, Woodruffe, Wuderope, Herb Walter

Gender: Hot

Planet: Mars

Element: Fire

Assoc. Deities: Ares, Mars, Thor, Horus

Parts Used: The herb

Basic Power: Purification

Specific Uses: Wonderfully fragrant; acquires its scent only as it dries. Much used in perfumery and bath herb mixtures. An herb of the Spring, used to clear away the closeness and drab atmosphere of the winter months. Carry when wishing to turn over a new leaf, or to change your outlook in life, especially in the spring. Added to the May Wine, the traditional witches' drink at Beltane. Brings victory to those who carry it.

Wormwood (Artemisia absinthium)

Folk Names: Old Woman, Absinthe, Absinth, Crown for a King

Gender: Hot

Planet: Mars, sometimes the Moon

Element: Air

Assoc. Deities: Diana, Isis, Artemis

Parts Used: The herb

Basic Powers: Clairvoyance, Protection

Specific Uses: Very magical herb sacred to the Moon. Used in love charms, as incense on All Hallows Eve, and in charms and incenses for evocation, scrying, divination, prophecy, and astral projection. Once burned in all incenses designed to raise spirits, now used in clairvoyance and divinatory incenses (especially in combination with mugwort) as well as in exorcism and protection blends. Throw onto fires on Samhain (Halloween) to gain protection from the spirits roaming the night. Burn while using a pendulum.

Yarrow (Achillea millefolium)

Folk Names: Seven Year's Love, Sanguinary, Old Man's Mustard, Military Herb, Old Man's Pepper, Soldier's Woundwort, Knight's Milfoil, Nosebleed, Thousand Seal, Hundred-Leaved Grass, Millefolium, Milfoil, Arrow Root, Eerie, Ladies' Mantle, Knyghten, Wound Wort, Stanch Weed, Field Hops, Tansy, Gearwe, Noble Yarrow, Yarroway, Devil's Bit, Devil's Plaything, Achillea, Snake's Grass, Death Flower, Stanch Griss

Gender: Cold

Planet: Venus

Element: Water

Assoc. Deities: Venus, Aphrodite, Hathor, Freya

Parts Used: Flowers

Basic Powers: Love, Clairvoyance, Exorcism

Specific Uses: Used in divination spells and to consult the I Ching. Sleeping with a bag of yarrow under one's pillow gives dreams of one's future spouse. Was a witches' herb, used in many other love and marriage charms, as it has the power to keep a couple together happily for 7 years. Worn as an amulet, it wards off negativity. Held in the hand it stops all fear. It is sometimes added to exorcism incenses. Considered a sacred plant with spiritual qualities by the Chinese.

Yew (Taxus baccata)

Folk Names: Chinwood, English Yew, European Yew

Gender: Cold

Planet: Saturn

Element: Earth

<u>Lotus</u> (Nymphaea odorata, N. lotus, or Zizyphus lotus)

Folk Names: Water lily, White Pond Lily, Water Cabbage, Cow Cabbage

Gender: Cold

Planet: Moon

Element: Water

Assoc. Deities: Isis, Khensu, Hecate, Neith, Selene

Parts Used: Rootstock, flowers

Basic Powers: Fertility, Visions, Magic

Specific Uses: Revered by the Egyptians. Represents the Goddess Isis and human fertility. Flowers used in perfumery. Root is POISONOUS.

<u>Lovage</u> (Levisticum officinale)

Folk Names: Love Root, Lavose, Sea Parsley, Italian Parsley, Loving Herbs, Love Parsley, Lubestico, Levistticum, Chinese Lovage

Gender: Hot

Planet: Sun

Element: Water

Assoc. Deities: Isis, Diana, Brigid

Parts Used: Root

Basic Powers: Love, Purification

Specific Uses: Root in the bath refreshes one psychically and makes one more attractive to the opposite sex. Carry as a love attractor.

<u>Mace</u>: See Nutmeg.

<u>Magic Mushrooms</u> (Psilocybe mexicana) See Amanita and Fly Agaric

Folk Names: Death Cap, Death Angel

Gender: Cold

Planet: Saturn

Element: Earth

Assoc. Deities: Hecate, Nephthys, Isis, Ceridwen, Saturn

Parts Used: The mushroom, POISONOUS

Basic Powers: Prophecy, Visions

Specific Uses: These hallucinogenic mushrooms are used by Indians and others for visions, to see the future, advice, and to communicate with spirits and ghosts. They should be gathered under the new moon before dawn with a proper ritual.